Aaron's Story in Verse

The True Story of Our Brave, eight-year-old Little Man's Battle to Conquer Cancer.

A Lasting Tribute

Written by

DENNY SENIOR

Aaron's Dad

Aaron's Story In Verse

Authored by Denny Senior (Aaron's Dad)

www.marciampublishing.com

Acknowledgements

✪

To complete this book, a lasting tribute to my son, there are so many people to thank and acknowledge. These are:

AARON - The man himself. He was so unique, with so many attributes, this warrants his story to be written. It's just so sad he is not here to read his story of survival.

TO ALL THE STAFF FROM THE CONSULTANTS TO DOMESTICS AT THE BIRMINGHAM CHILDREN'S HOSPITAL - Their dedication to the cause of attending to children with so many illnesses, including our son, deserves nothing but the highest praise.

TO OUR FAMILY AND FRIENDS - For their loyal support throughout this crisis in our lives.

TO AARON'S FRIENDS AND THEIR PARENTS - For taking time out in all kinds of weather to visit Aaron, ensuring our little man kept in touch with his friends.

TO THE BBC - For choosing Aaron to do his story; it gave him an alternative to the hospital routine, and for capturing him together with all his attributes on the screen.

TO THE TEACHERS AND CHILDREN AT HOLLYFIELDS INFANT SCHOOL - For their letters, visits and support throughout this devastating time.

TO THE CHILDREN AT HOLLYFIELDS JUNIOR SCHOOL - For their cards, letters and fundraising on behalf of Aaron for the Birmingham Children's Hospital Appeal Fund.

TO THE BEAVERS, CUB SCOUTS AND THEIR LEADERS - For their support, visits, presents and, most of all, for making Aaron feel he was still part of the troop, while in hospital, highlighted by his "swim up" ceremony from Beavers to Cub Scouts. This was so important to maintain Aaron's spirit and motivation.

TO THE STAFF AND MANAGEMENT AT CHAPLIN BROS. - For allowing my wife so much time off work to be with our son. Your support is greatly appreciated.

TO THE STAFF AND MANAGEMENT AT CLEONE FOODS LTD. - For allowing me the flexibility in hours of work, to be there for my son when needed.

TO ALL THE VIEWERS WHO HAVE WRITTEN TO US - Your letters since the series finished have touched our hearts and made us so proud of our son that he has touched so many people. These letters give us so much comfort in our time of grief, just to realise there are so many people out there who have us in their thoughts.

Finally, to all the people who are part of the above and mentioned in the verses and shown in the pictures. Thank you for contributing to the story lines. Where necessary pseudonyms names are used for anonymity.

About The Author

I am Aaron's dad, approaching the ripe old age of seventy-four. I wrote this book some 25 years ago as I was approaching my fifties. I was then employed as a Manager in a food manufacturing company. I am now retired.

As far back as my school days, writing has always seemed to be one of my strengths, with the ability to describe scenes and situations vividly. I started writing verses in my teens, mainly for girlfriends on birthdays and other special occasions. I have always had the desire to write a book of verses and commenced writing a book approximately thirty years ago. The contents were to encompass my life, from emigrating to England in 1957 from Jamaica at the age of seven. Although I have written a few pages, I haven't yet completed the book. Maybe one day, with Aaron's inspiration, I will finish this book.

I continued to write verses throughout my life, when inspired by events that have occurred. These included things like the birth of my children, deaths of close relatives, including my father, and marriages where I have been a best man or a spokesperson. Among my family I have gained a reputation for writing verses, and it has become expected of me to write verses when a special or moving event occurs.

Regarding writing this book, the inspiration came from the most devastating event in our family, which was the death of our eight-year-old son, Aaron, due to cancer, on July 13th, 1998. That period in our lives is in our memory forever, because knowing your only son is dying and having to wait and watch him die is by far the worst experience any family has to endure. I can't imagine anything in the future being as traumatic as that period in our lives. Yet from the depths of sorrow this book has emerged. It started by me writing my eulogy for his funeral. The favourable comments from the mourners encouraged me to continue writing and made me decide to treat Aaron's death in a positive way. This gave me a new purpose in life in trying to overcome this tragedy and greatly assisted me in coping with the grieving process. It could be said that without me writing this book, the motivation to continue to try to live a full and purposeful life would have been extremely difficult.

Aaron's bravery touched many people during the last months of his short life, with him becoming a source of inspiration for others. His concern for other children was at times greater than being concerned for himself, therefore one of the legacies he has left behind is for me to try to help other children. If this book, achieves this legacy in terms of overcoming adversity or is inspirational in their lives, I would personally feel I am continuing Aaron's work.

Finally, although such a personal tragedy has realised my ambition of writing a book of verses, which fills me with so much sadness, by using adversity in a positive manner, for me it is a means of trying to come to terms with such a huge loss. It will ensure Aaron will never be forgotten by many people. His inspirational qualities will live on and on, which means he hasn't died in vain.

Introduction

T his compilation of verses are based on a turning point in our family life which evolved between September 1997 and July 1998.

During this period, our seven-year-old son, Aaron, was taken seriously ill with a rare form of the cancer known as Non-Hodgkin lymphoma. Although he fought long and hard to beat this dreaded disease, he finally succumbed to the illness and passed away on July 13th 1998. His death has given me the inspiration to write this story, expressing my feelings and the events of the last year in these verses.

They cover all emotions from happiness to sadness, reflecting the roller coaster ride we have experienced. We believe whoever reads this story will appreciate how parents feel in these circumstances and gain strength in their own life, regardless of their current situation. We also hope it will inspire other people who are in a similar environment, to give them the strength to cope and relate to what we have gone through.

These verses are how I remembered this sad journey in our lives. Where necessary pseudonyms names are used for anonymity.

Background

We were a normal family of four living in a typical semi-detached house in the suburbs of Birmingham. Our daughter of eighteen was just about to start university, which was meant to be a happy moment in our family life. Unfortunately, the inception of Aaron's illness was the day we were taking her to university.

Therefore, what was meant to be a happy but emotional day turned into one that will remain in our memory forever. With Aaron being taken ill, the emphasis reversed from our daughter to our son, simply because the symptoms he was showing appeared very serious in our eyes.

This resulted in a normal family life being turned upside down for nine months. Aaron was to spend the majority of the time in the Birmingham Children's Hospital with his mother. She had to give up work, to be beside him, just to be there for him, to give him support whenever it was needed. Our daughter was at university studying for her degree and dad needed to be the mainstay of this whole episode. This meant continuing to work, going to the hospital every day or evening and ensuring the normal factors that are necessary to maintain the running of the household were not forgotten.

As you can appreciate, this was an extremely difficult time in our life. It was to be a test of our mental strength, a test of survival, which sadly for our only son, it wasn't meant to be.

Contents

Aaron's Story in Verse

The True Story of Our Brave, eight-year-old Little Man's Battle to Conquer Cancer.

A Lasting Tribute

Written by

DENNY SENIOR
Aaron's Dad

Overview

The story starts with Aaron as a schoolboy and our last summer holiday on the Norfolk Broads, It is a place where we had never been, but always wanted to go. It was a typical family holiday in a chalet. Everything seemed ideal. We were looking forward to the future with Aaron, our little man, starting junior school and Theresa, our daughter, going off to university.

If we were clairvoyants and could foresee the future, we couldn't have been more wrong, because the forthcoming year was the most traumatic and was to be the worst living nightmare that any family can endure.

This story in verses describes in detail the experiences and heartaches we have gone through, when our son became seriously ill, to be finally diagnosed as having a very rare form of cancer known as Non-Hodgkin lymphoma. It covers from the first sign that something was wrong, the period of diagnosis, through to his eventual death and the after-effects that behold us after he passed away.

It encompasses his period in the Birmingham Children's Hospital, the treatment he had to undergo and the effect it had on our son and his family. It also epitomises the highs and lows that are part of having someone so very close suffering from cancer.

It highlights the humorous and very serious occasions when life or death was in the balance, also the many people we have encountered during this terrible, sad journey in our life, including other children and families who are in similar situations. The memorable period in hospital was him being selected for the BBC Children's Hospital series, to do "Aaron's Story". The filming of this series gave Aaron so much happiness and boosted his morale tremendously during such a period of adversity. His strong character, infectious personality and his sense of humour comes shining through on the screen for the world to see.

Sadly, he passed away before the series was televised, so he is not here to see himself on the screen as a TV star. We know in life's cycle you really have no control over your destiny, but for our family it is comforting to know he didn't die in vain; he has left behind a visual legacy and so many treasured memories that will never fade away.

Finally, it could be said that in the eight years he has spent on this earth, he has achieved more than some people achieve in eighty. Therefore, the final verse in this book, "Aaron Final Message From Above", the TV series and this book of verses covering the last year of his life, can be considered an appropriate conclusion and a fitting tribute to the life of this exceptional little man.

Aaron The Schoolboy

Aaron started Hollyfields Infant School back in 1994
His academic life commencing, somewhere he has never been before
He settled in, with the other children and teachers he was soon very popular
Early indications were, he had the potential to be a very bright scholar

We became aware of his potential at the very first parents' evening
When his teacher told us, you have an exceptional child in the making
We were surprised, we didn't realise our son was that good, that clever
Those words, we still remember, they are in our memory forever

He continued to develop and was always in the top two of his class
The tests he had taken, he would never fail, always achieving a pass
His ability to learn, was unquestionable, he was becoming a real student
His brains were his strength, it could be seen, it was clearly evident

The little girls all wanted to be his friend, he had this magical appeal
His magnetism was there to be seen, you could almost touch it, it was real
On sports day, he would seem to roll along, not run like a true athlete
He had been chubby from birth, maybe it made it difficult to pick up his feet

You can take him or leave him, but you won't forget him, that's for certain
He acted in the school plays, with a part to play, always willing to entertain
His memory was unbelievable, he could remember all his class mate's birthdays
From the announcement in assembly, it would stay in his memory always

JULY 1997
AARON IN HIS SCHOOL PLAY AS THE BIG BAD WOLF
DISGUISED AS THE GRANDMOTHER IN RED RIDING HOOD

Hollyfield Infant School

This is to certify that

Aaron

scored

96

in our Sponsored Spell 1997

AARON'S CERTIFICATE
FOR SPELLING 96 WORDS OUT OF 100 CORRECTLY
IN A SPONSORED SPELLING CONTEST

AARON THE SCHOOLBOY

I can remember taking him to the discos, on a Friday night at the school
He would stroll in, wander around, surveying the scene, he was Mr Cool
To the little girls, looking out for him, he would get an instant reaction
They would say "Hello Aaron" hoping for a piece of his dancing action

He would be dancing away in a group, gyrating to the rhythm of the beat
So smooth, so natural, you could hardly see the movement of his feet
He had this coolness about him, he might even give the impression he was shy
This certainly wasn't true, that is the style of Aaron, so loveable to the eye

At times he would be talking too much, that is why he was "Mr Know-It-All"
Sometimes he would get into trouble for this, he had to stand against the wall
He was forever asking awkward questions, putting the teachers on the spot
Diplomacy was never his strength, with Aaron what you see is what you got

In his final year at the infant school, he passed with flying colours
Now a new adventure is waiting in September, he has to move up to the Juniors
New teachers to meet, older children, he will be starting all over again
With his attitude, it shouldn't be a problem, it shouldn't cause any real pain

The Beginning

It was August 1997. We went to Norfolk for our family holiday
Little did we know it would turn out to be such a memorable stay
We played football, built sandcastles and paddled in the sea
Since then our life has turned upside down, we could never foresee

At his new school, he was complaining of headaches by late September
His mum thought, he needed his eyes tested. It was due, she remembered
Dad thought, he now has to work harder in the juniors, using his brain
In the infants, he was top of the class, it was easier, not causing any pain

Then a telephone call to work from his school, saying Aaron wasn't very well
I went to the school to fetch him, he had a headache and a dizzy spell
We took him to our doctor, he thought the pain was due to an infection
He gave him some medicine, we thought he will soon be back in action

We were due to take his sister to check into university on the Saturday
Due to his pains, we were in two minds whether to take him with us that day
We took a chance, his sister was leaving home, the first time on her own
It was a risk, what came next, it was impossible for us to have ever known

Aaron became hysterical in the car, screaming, it was so frightening
We started to worry, he was out of control, it seems he was hallucinating
We dashed to Milton Keynes, the nearest hospital, in a state of fright
Hoping the doctors could diagnose what was wrong and shed some light

He was quickly admitted, given an examination and had a brain scan
We waited patiently in the children's ward, with our little man
They inserted needles, gave him antibiotics, extracted blood to test
As parents, we were worried, trying to be calm, praying for the best

We were in the hands of the doctors and nurses, we feel so helpless
Not knowing what was wrong, what has he got, what is his illness
The results of the scan came through, indicating his brain was clear
First hurdle, first signs of relief, to know there is nothing there

He had to be still, a lumbar puncture, for analysis was required
It was impossible, he was frantic, he screamed and just cried
We comforted and cuddled him, trying hard to calm him down
He wouldn't have the needle, no, no, he kept saying with a frown

They gave up, hoping the other tests would prove more conclusive
When Aaron says no, he means no, that's him, he's so very decisive
Being away from home, they weren't sure what to do, what to plan
The answer was simple, we will do whatever is best for our little man

Due to the intravenous needle in his wrist, he developed an infection
That made it worse, he was in agony, it was now total rejection
The other parents couldn't look, they themselves could feel the pain
They tried to remove the needle, we had to keep him under restrain

They managed to remove the needle and inserted it in the other wrist
He was under anaesthetic, the needle he feared, he would still resist
This experience gave him a fear of needles, he would just panic
At the sight of a needle, he would be screaming, he would be frantic

We spent four days in the hospital, sleeping in a chair at night
Waiting for the results of the tests, praying they will be all right
Finally the results came through: it was mycoplasma, a virus
With antibiotics, it should clear up, it was such a relief to us

Finally, we were allowed to return home, it was a Wednesday
Our first experience of Milton Keynes wasn't a pleasant stay
We thanked the doctors and nurses for their help and said farewell
Happy to be going home, although the future you can never tell

We headed northwards to Birmingham, our home port of call
Feeling confident, he will be back at school in no time at all
We were so glad to be back home, we felt a sense of relief
Thinking the nightmare was over, that was our true belief

We soon realised how wrong we were, thinking we were winning
We were lulled into a false sense of security, it was just beginning
What was to come in the next year, will change our lives forever
The experiences that were to come, will never go, they will never

Back Home

─────────⭐─────────

Back home, in our familiar environment, getting back into the old routine
Mum and Dad taking turns to look after him, to give him his medicine
As the days went by, he didn't appear to be making any progress
He wasn't like the Aaron we knew, he seemed so lethargic, so lifeless

We took him to our doctor and explained the symptoms he was showing
He said it was the virus, it does take time before he will be glowing
But we need to go to our local hospital, he will make an appointment
A few more days went by and there were still no signs of improvement

He was sweating profusely, started itching and continually scratching
Worried, we took him to the Children's Hospital early Monday morning
The doctor went through the process of a neurological examination
The signs were positive, "It's the effects of the virus" was the explanation

They gave us medicine to ease the itching, to make him more comfortable
We had to return a week later, "Please bring him back if he is not stable"
We went back home still feeling uneasy, not relaxed about the situation
Thinking there is still worse to come, just put it down to parents' intuition

We were right, we weren't happy, he was now having problems walking
He was having problems passing water, he was having problems sleeping
We took him back to the hospital, hoping they could put our mind at rest
Another doctor, same story explained, then went through the same test

After consultation with another doctor, the reason was still this virus
We weren't really happy, some more drugs, it didn't seem right to us
We took him home again, hoping he would show signs of progressing
It wasn't to be, he was just the same, if anything, he was regressing

We took him back again, this time determined to have him admitted
Another new doctor, same examination, same story, again transmitted
He was suggesting we took him home again, we weren't happy by far
We wanted to see the original doctor, apparently she was a registrar

After a long wait she came, did some tests and decided to admit Aaron
We were relieved, at least this time we might find out what's wrong
They found a bed on ward nine, he couldn't walk, he had to go in a wheelchair
We didn't know, it was the start of a long period of breathing hospital air

The Diagnosis

The paediatric consultant came, the symptoms, he needed to know
Apart from his problems passing water, it was like walking on dough
This seemed extremely serious, an MRI scan was done the next day
The results came through very quickly, Oh! What did they have to say?

My wife immediately called me from work for the result of the scan
Although my mind was in turmoil, I had to be strong, be a man
The news was what we had always feared, we didn't want to hear
He had tumours on his spine, on his brain, our worst nightmare

My wife and I clasped our hands, we couldn't hold back the tears
Thinking why us? Why our little man? Why this, in his innocent years?
They left us alone for a while, just to cry, to gain some composure
We thought, is death around the corner? We just couldn't be sure

They came to tell us what was needed, some spinal fluid for analysis
This required a lumbar puncture, to try to obtain a diagnosis
We were in a trance, trying hard to listen, not really comprehending
We were devastated, in a state of shock, having difficulty understanding

We then had to compose ourselves, trying to be strong, to tell Aaron
He is intelligent, so inquisitive, he needed to know, what was going on
The consultant carefully explained to him what was causing his illness
He needed a lumbar puncture, he would be asleep and it would be painless

That same day we had to tell our family, they were all in deep sorrow
The dreaded word cancer, always gives a feeling, there is no tomorrow
Mavis, a friend from work, she was concerned, came that same evening
I took her outside to explain, my emotions surfaced, I just started crying

She hugged me, trying to console me, saying he will be all right, don't worry
She was trying to be emotionally strong, saying, "I am sorry Denny, so sorry"
I managed to compose myself, I had to be there, for my wife, for my son
There could be a long road ahead, which could keep going on, going on

Aaron's fear of needles, he thought it was Milton Keynes all over again
He was not happy, we tried to convince him it would be free from pain
In theatre they put some magic cream on his arm to numb the surface
He saw the needle, he was frightened, struggling, the fear on his face

They restrained him, inserted the needle, he went out like a light
They did the operation, woke him up, his face was not a happy sight
When he realised it was all over, while asleep, he didn't feel a thing
He was a lot happier, maybe next time it won't be quite so frightening

His sister was still at university, how do you explain the illness to her?
She came home at the weekend, in a quiet room we all sat down together
We briefed her, she found it difficult to understand, to comprehend
"He is going to be alright, isn't he?" she said. We are sorry we don't know the end

She became emotional, it was her only brother, it's understandable
We tried to comfort her, tried to reassure her, tried to make her stable
We told her it could be a long road ahead, we all need to be strong
Aaron needs to believe he will recover, there is nothing seriously wrong

The results of the lumbar puncture came through it wasn't conclusive
They needed to do a biopsy operation on his spine, to be more positive
We were transferred to the post theatre ward, Aaron wasn't very pleased
He had become accustomed to the nurses, especially the ones he had teased

As he was being booked into ward one, he was being cheeky as usual
"This is not like ward nine, the nurses are better," his voice so casual
The nurse smiling, probably thinking! We have got a right one here!
It was an Irish nurse, he wanted to know, where she came from, from where

Aaron is a very inquisitive child who likes to give people the third degree
A mind of information, he needs to know everything, he will not let it be
He goes on and on, wanting to know every detail, he just won't let it go
Until he is completely satisfied, it is his nature, he feels he needs to know

With his upfront style, sense of humour, he soon settled into the ward
Keeping the nurses on their toes, Aaron is not slow in coming forward
It did not take long before he became the central figure in ward one
He realised the nurses were fine, he was making friends with everyone

We went with him to theatre for the biopsy, he was a bit apprehensive
They injected a sleeping drug into his wrist, he was fine very passive
They performed the operation, removed some sample tissues for analysis
The surgeon said it went well, now we have to wait for a diagnosis

He came back from theatre in a relaxed, subdued mood, looking fine
Unfortunately the after-effects of having an operation on your spine
Is that you are bedridden for five days, not being able to move
He was on painkillers, he wasn't very happy, he didn't really approve

It was such a difficult time, not knowing, just hoping he is in the clear
It took about four days for the result, this is what you call living in fear
The consultant took us to a quiet room, it appears the tumours are benign
This means they are not cancerous, is this a negative or a positive sign

The tumours still have to be removed, although you are a little more relieved
A course of steroids, hopefully this will help the problem, you try to believe
He commenced the treatment, gradually you could see some improvement
He was walking better, passing water easier, it was a positive development

The effect of the steroids made his body enlarge and it bloated his face
But if it was making him better, we didn't mind, if it gets us out of this place
It affected his appetite, he was always eating, to us, a positive reaction
Soon his walking was improving, we are hoping, soon he will be back in action

Marion, one of his nurses, when he was on ward nine, was a regular visitor
He was very cheeky towards her, yet she grew fond of Aaron the inquisitor
Paul the male nurse on the ward, they were friends, he became his mate
He was always telling him stories, having discussions, having a debate

After a couple of weeks, another MRI scan was required, to see the impact
Fingers and legs crossed, hoping it will be positive, this is not fiction, it's fact
The results came, the tumours had shrunk significantly and that's a blessing
Is he on the road to recovery? Is he going to be all right? We are only guessing

He continued to progress, he was his old self, walking like he was before
From a parents' viewpoint, we were so happy, we couldn't ask for more
He had improved so much, they decided he was fit enough to be discharged
We were glad to go home, although his bodily features were still enlarged

At home he was his normal self, considering he wasn't under any medication
We realised we were not in the clear, he will be back weekly for an examination
He will be at home, November the 20th is his birthday, he will be eight
He could have a few friends round, have a small party, he could celebrate

He had lots of presents, his pride and joy was his England football kit
His closest friends came round, he was really happy, he looked really fit
He was running around, playing, you wouldn't believe anything was wrong
Yet there was this underlying feeling, he wouldn't be at home for very long

A few days after his birthday, he started dragging his left leg once again
Our happiness was short lived, all we could feel inside was yet more pain
We knew the steroids weren't a cure, it was used for controlling the tumour
We took him back to hospital, it is getting serious, there is little humour

We are aware there is more to come, Aaron's illness was becoming a mystery
The doctors were baffled, they were consulting the best brains in the country
They gave him another course of steroids and kept him under observation
Just to control the tumour, keep him comfortable, see if there is any reaction

The steroids weren't making an impact, he was getting worse, progressively
All we could do was to be patient, be there for him, keep thinking positively
After a couple of weeks, still no improvement, another MRI scan needed to be done
He was injected with a dye that shows up abnormalities,
we are hoping there are none

**AARON WITH SOME OF HIS FRIENDS
AT HIS LAST BIRTHDAY PARTY,
HE WAS EIGHT YEARS OLD**

THE DIAGNOSIS

The results of the scans came through, it wasn't what we wanted to hear
It showed up tumours on his spine, on his brain, they were very clear
When compared with the previous scans, you could see they were significant
What happens next, another biopsy operation, just what we didn't want

The tumours on his spinal cord caused him to lose control of his bladder
To overcome this problem, he had a minor operation to fit a catheter
It affected his bowels, made him constipated, he needed enemas for relief
All this for Aaron was embarrassing, for him it was nothing but grief

By this time Christmas was coming up, home is where we wanted to be
We weren't sure if it would be possible, we will just have to wait and see
He had the operation, another sample sent to the laboratory for analysis
There was us hoping on this occasion, they will find a conclusive diagnosis

Aaron started thinking about Christmas presents, telling us what he wanted
A PlayStation was top of the list, he will have to wait to see if this was granted
The only present our family wanted was to have Aaron home fit and well
That was our only wish from day one, will it come true? You never can tell!

Aaron's condition was deteriorating, the next major crisis wasn't far away
Out of the blue, his mum, voice trembling, phoned me at work one day
Can you come right away, Aaron is losing his speech, he is incoherent
I dashed to the hospital, thinking, this is all too much, for one so innocent

I got there, my son was trying hard to talk, the words wouldn't come out
It was difficult to understand him, he was frustrated, he wanted to shout
He was frightened, not knowing what was going on, you could see his fears
His mum, his favourite nurse Clariss, were caressing him, almost in tears

It appears he was having a massive fit, caused by the tumour on his brain
Dr Jameson his surgeon came quickly, the tumour may be inflamed, he explained
They gave him some anti-fit medicine, to attempt to reduce the inflammation
He quickly arranged to have a CT scan on his brain, to obtain confirmation

By the time the scan was due, he had slipped into a state of unconsciousness
We were really scared, thinking are we losing him? Our little man was lifeless
During the scan, he was dribbling from his mouth, I was trying to understand

What is really happening to us, with tear-filled eyes, I grasped my son's hand

The X-ray showed his brain tumour was surrounded by a circle of inflammation
That is why he is unconscious, it is the root cause of his current condition
It was becoming critical, really serious, he needed to go into intensive care
They managed to find a bed for him, in his comatose state, he was taken there

His brain was overworked, he needed to be put to sleep, his brain needed a rest
They wired him up, they connected him to a ventilator, we hoped for the best
We had to leave the ward while this was being done, it is not a pretty sight
Seeing your son being inserted with tubes, wires, can give you quite a fright

We waited patiently in a private room unable to relax or feel comfortable
When it was over we went to see him, it wasn't pleasant, but he was stable
It was so terrifying, seeing your son unconscious, with monitors everywhere
Your mental state in turmoil, wondering if he will survive this latest scare

Family and friends were there for us, trying to support us through the distress
They could see how we felt, they knew we were under severe mental stress
We were advised to go home, there is nothing we can do, just try to sleep
He will be nursed on a one-to-one basis all night, just believe he is asleep

We took their advice, although we were reluctant to leave our little man
They would ring us if there were any changes, try to sleep the best you can
At home, it was difficult, we couldn't rest, we had another sleepless night
Wondering if he will come out of the darkness to once again see daylight

We returned to the hospital early next morning, still feeling drained mentally
Not knowing that today our emotions will fluctuate from joy to despair totally
He was still asleep, looking so peaceful, it was so difficult for me and my wife
At about midday, he will come off the ventilator to be brought back to life

THE DIAGNOSIS

Once again we couldn't watch, as he regained consciousness, became awake
In the same room we waited, hoping he will be ok, all this is so hard to take
They called us in, it was time to see him, he is fine, thank God, what a relief
So happy to hear him talking, although in a whisper, sheer joy beyond belief

He was wondering what had happened to him, he has lost 24 hours, a day
He was soon making up for lost time, talking non-stop, so much he had to say
We had to explain what had happened, why it was necessary for him to sleep
To us it was another scare along the road, another sad memory for us to keep

Maggie his teacher came. He asked her for a book on big cats and an atlas
She said, it's the first time from intensive care, she has had such a request
This is just another example of our son, demonstrating his true uniqueness
At least this proves he still has his faculties intact, his mental awareness

Dr Stevenson the consultant wanted to see us, we are thinking is this bad news?
My wife, me, my sister went into a quiet room, waiting to hear his views
He said, we have a diagnosis from the biopsy, I am afraid it is not very good
He has a cancer known as Non-Hodgkin lymphoma, explaining the best he could

It was very unusual and complicated, that is why the diagnosis took so long
We were in a state, although we always felt something was seriously wrong
The tumours on his spine and his brain are malignant, they are cancerous
He said he would explain in more detail later, now it is him we have to trust

We were left alone, to try to understand, comprehend, what we have been told
We were emotional, thinking will he be able to beat this disease? We must be bold
The only relief after months of torment is we finally know what's wrong with him
We have to be positive, believe we will win, believe his chances are more than slim

Eventually we had to go back to our son, he now needs us more than ever
We would have to explain to Aaron, you can't fool him, he is too clever
After a few of hours in intensive care, he was well enough to be released.
He returned to his ward, still talking, glad to see his favourite nurse, Clairiss

BRAVERY CERTIFICATE

Awarded to Aaron Senior

on Saturday 13th December

Well done for being brave when you had your blood taken
Love Andrea

A BRAVERY CERTIFICATE PRESENTED TO AARON

The Plan of Action

That evening, Dr Stevenson took us into a quiet room to explain the situation
My sister also came, she was a nurse she could understand the plan of action
He was very considerate, appreciating that we are under a tremendous strain
Therefore, he took time out to express his sorrow, trying to minimise the pain

He explained the circumstances of the disease and why it was in a rare form
We thought that's just typical of Aaron, so different, not wishing to conform
It was the location of the tumours, it was unusual, making it difficult to detect
Once again we were thinking, that is our little man, it is what we should expect

He recalled it has been a long time since he has seen a cancer of this nature
Now we have to follow a protocol to try to cure it, there is a set structure
He remarked that this type of cancer normally can be extremely aggressive
He will have to undergo very intensive chemotherapy to make it regressive

He forewarned us of the side effects that may occur from the treatment
Like liver, kidney problems, loss of hair, all this sounds so unpleasant
It is also possible that he may be infertile, when he becomes an adult
We will have to take each day as it comes and pray for a positive result

The treatment destroys good and bad cells, so he will need blood transfusions
The cells need to be replaced, so that he can maintain a strong constitution
He will need this, to enable him to continue the treatment through to the end
We will need supporting, it is on the doctors and nurses we have to depend

He will need to be in hospital during the full course of the chemo treatment
His appetite may go, he may need a nasal gastric feed to give him nourishment
It is also possible, the cancer, the drugs, could leave a permanent disability
He could be wheelchair bound, losing his independence, losing his mobility

The treatment takes six months to follow the recognised procedure
All we were thinking, as a family we have to be strong for him, that is for sure
Our main questions are; what is the prognosis? What are his chances of living?
He was non-committal, too many unknowns, to give his chances of surviving

We were having difficulty grasping all what's being said, a typical reaction
He then proceeded to describe to us what was necessary, the plan of action
He will have a mild dosage of chemotherapy, to start the treatment, initially
Then it will be very heavy dosages, to attack the cancerous cells, very quickly

We have to prepare ourselves for the worst outcome and hope for the best
The next six months will put our mental and physical resolve to the test
Hoping and praying the treatment works and he comes through feeling better
Our main concern is survival, that's all we can wish for as a mother and father

Each stage is known as a block and takes about five days to administer
Then there is a break of two to three weeks, to give his body time to recover
He will have a variety of drugs to nullify the effects of the chemotherapy
On his other bodily functions, he will also need extensive physiotherapy

He will have ongoing tests, examinations and MRI scans periodically
We will do everything possible to ensure we maintain his body physically
A central line has to be fitted into his chest, into his bloodstream, directly
This is to feed the drugs, so they have a maximum impact, very quickly

Some drugs are injected directly into his spine, by lumbar puncture
Listening to all Aaron has to go through is sheer torture
We realise the tumours need to be shrunk quickly, before they spread
Unfortunately, we have no choice in the matter, if not he could be dead

We will have to start the treatment as soon as possible, as soon as he is able
We asked if he could go home for Christmas, sorry, this wouldn't be possible
He can stay here over the Christmas, then he will be transferred to ward five
The specialist oncology ward, we are all praying he comes through this alive

After hearing what is going to occur, mentally we were in a state of confusion
It seems all unreal, it seems unbelievable, all a bad dream, all like an illusion
Sadly we come to our senses, realising we have to face reality, it isn't fiction
Now we have to go and see our little man, to tell him the news, the plan of action

Dr Stevenson was debating how to tell Aaron what he needs to go through
They tell children the truth, to gain their confidence, they all depend on you
With his experience, he carefully explained the diagnosis, the action required
All geared to make you better, "Can I go home for Christmas?" Aaron enquired

Apologetically, he told him it wouldn't be possible, a really sad thing to say
He had to start the treatment as quickly as possible, in fact the very next day
Aaron wasn't very happy, he explained Christmas in hospital is not too bad
All your presents will be here, you will still be with your sister, mum and dad

Dr Stevenson was brilliant, he soon realised Aaron is a very intelligent lad
You can't fool him, his mind is very advanced, that's why all this is so very sad
He said he will be back the next day to explain anything, we can't think of now
As usual Aaron had to ask him one last question, that's him, as we all know

The Immediate After-Effects

The immediate after-effects of hearing such terrible news is mind-blowing
So many things go through your mind, mentally you are overflowing
Is he going to live or die? That is the question, it is uppermost in your mind
We look at him trying to hold back the tears, an answer, you cannot find

We have come this far, thinking positively, now we face our biggest test
We have been running on adrenaline, unable to feel relaxed, unable to rest
Our little man has been through so much, now he has to endure even more
It is so heartbreaking, wondering if he will be able to cope like he did before

We are trying to come to terms with our immediate future, what lies ahead
Fate has dealt us a savage blow, 1998 is what we now dread
We need to tell his sister the bad news, it won't be easy, with her living away
She is coming home for Christmas, so sad, it certainly won't be a happy stay

He now needs us more than ever, our sole objective is to be here for our son
We must keep his morale at a high level, it will be tough, but we must soldier on
Our strong family bond will give us the strength, we are all in this together
All for one, one for all, that will be our motto, he is our son, he is a brother

His mum will live at the hospital, she won't leave him, that's for sure
Dad will still need to work, our family will be apart, we will be under pressure
Life still goes on outside the hospital, the household still has to be maintained
It is going to be a real test of character, it isn't a shower, it has really rained

To keep him happy, we will be able to get him a special Christmas gift
It may be his last on earth, we must do whatever is possible, to give him a lift
We will have to find him a PlayStation, at the moment they are like gold dust
Friends, family, are scouring the shops, they are out there looking for us

That is the present he wants the most, it is top of his Christmas shopping list
We must not let him down, that is what he requested, that is what he insists
Luckily, through a friend, we managed to obtain this essential present
We didn't wait, he had it before Christmas Day, as if it was heaven-sent

He was so happy, he got what he wanted, his smile removed the darkness
For a while we forgot the future, for a short period we could relieve the stress
Now we have to make the most of spending Christmas day on the ward
Hoping next year we are at home, although we know, it is going to be hard

Christmas In Hospital

His sister has now come home from university, for the Christmas break
We have to tell her the bad news, it is going to be so hard for her to take
Once again we went to a quiet room, telling her she needs to be brave
Aaron has a serious life-threatening illness, but is a life they hope to save

Screaming out, "He is not going to die is he?" she is finding it hard to believe
We understand how she feels; he is her brother, what sad words to receive
We try to tell her, there is still a long way to go, she must remain positive
Aaron must be aware there is a future for him, we must not be negative

We explained to her the chemotherapy to be undertaken was very intensive
The treatment can also give complications, these can also be very extensive
We could see she was having difficulty taking all this in, it is understandable
With having to spend Christmas in hospital, all so unreal, all so unstable

We have cancelled our traditional family Christmas, due to Aaron's situation
It is now only for our son, to make him happy, to make it a special occasion
He may not be here to enjoy next Christmas, we don't know, that is what we fear
It is out of our hands, we have no control over his future, no control over next year

He commenced his treatment on Friday, three days before Christmas Day
Dr Stevenson came around to see if there was anything we wanted to know or say
Basically there is not a lot to say, the one answer we want, we cannot obtain
That is, is he going to live or die, a positive answer would help to ease the pain

During this period, Aaron awoke one night screaming hysterically and crying
He was shouting I want to go back to 1997, it was frightening
It scared his mum and his nurse, they were wondering, what was happening
His eyes were fixed, staring, as they tried to calm him down, stop him crying

When he finally calmed down, it appeared he had a bad dream or a nightmare

He started telling his mum, his nurse, the dream, his eyes showing some fear
He is in a room split into two halves, he was vividly explaining the scene
A man with a walking stick was with Granddad, the one he has never seen

He was with dad in the other half, he went across to Granddad, my father
He wanted Aaron to stop with him, he will protect him, they will be together
Aaron said he didn't want to, he wanted to go back to 1997
It was really strange, they have never met, maybe the dream was in heaven

His mum explained to his nurse that his Granddad died in 1985
This dream played havoc with our minds, wondering, if he is going to survive
His mum also recalled, one day before he was ill, she was taken by surprise
Aaron asked her, if she was going to bury him or cremate him, when he dies

She just replied, "It is you that should bury me, you shouldn't ask such a question"
You don't want to say it, but you do think, maybe he is having a premonition
You put it to the back of your mind, hoping it is not an omen for the future
If it were to happen, we would be devastated, our life would be sheer torture

The other strange thing is that the dream occurred when Christmas is in the air
When the thought of Jesus is prominent, he is all around us, he is everywhere
You can't help but think about, how uncanny, how scary all this appears
We are hoping he has no more dreams like this, hoping they all disappear

That episode is now over, we are looking forward to Christmas Day
He will have lots of presents, we are hoping he will be able to play
We are trying to take one day at a time, trying not to look too far ahead
Trying not to think that this time next year, our little man could be dead

Christmas Day arrives, Santa Claus comes with his sack to do his ward round
With presents for the little children with smiling faces, new friends he has found
We also have to smile and look forward, not back, what has gone has gone
Make the most of what we have today, enjoy each day with our precious one

Presents arrive from our family and friends, there are so many to open
It is certainly a special Christmas for Aaron, let's hope it is not an omen
He is surrounded by so many toys and games, he is spoilt for choice
His little cousins are all here to play with him, laughing, making a noise

The hospital staff, were excellent, making us at ease and feeling so welcome
We had Christmas dinner as a family, in some ways it was home from home
We enjoyed the day the best we could, considering our current mental state
The next day he will be moved to oncology, his new home for ninety-eight

CRASH THUNDER

Found on Aaron's computer after his passing.

The Treatment,
The First Phase

─────────── ★ ───────────

It was like moving house, as we were transferred, with him in a wheelchair
Aaron wasn't very happy at having to move again, he said, "It's just not fair"
He was moaning all the way to his new ward, he just kept going on and on
He had become accustomed to the staff and made many friends on ward one

The nurses explained that they will still come to see him and keep in touch
Especially the male nurse Paul, they have had many a debate and talked so much
He became a right pain to a nurse on ward five, his mum felt sorry for her
She had to apologise to Sheila the Sister, she said, "It shows he is a fighter"

He was introduced to Caron his named nurse, as he gradually calmed down
He didn't take to her immediately, his facial expression still showed a frown
The room he was in contained four beds, a couple of cots, it was so congested
It is something we have to get used to, our patience will be sorely tested

The first step in the process was to get his central line inserted into his chest
He has to go down to theatre, he would be put to sleep, he could have a rest
He liked going to theatre, because he loved having the gas, to knock him out
He loved the sensation as he drifted off to dreamland, without even a shout

He now has to start the heavy chemo treatment, geared to getting him better
We hope he responds positively, our feeling for him has never been greater
We are worried about the side effects, we know they can be really serious
If they are not counteracted quickly, we could lose the one who is so precious

Before the treatment starts, he needs a series of tests, you can't take a chance
They need to ensure his body is physically ready, for this test of endurance

The results come through, he is in good shape, he is ready to go, he is fine
The first drug, requires a lumbar puncture, to inject directly into his spine

Other drugs have to be fed through his central line, gradually at a preset rate
You look at him lying there surrounded by lines, so much he has to tolerate
He also requires fluids fed continuously, to prevent his body dehydrating
Now we can appreciate, what is really ahead, at times it will be frustrating

All we can do now is watch and wait, just be there to give him encouragement
Try to maintain his morale, his motivation, to come through all this treatment
We are trying to think of what we can do to give him a boost occasionally
Whatever is possible, we will attempt to do, to keep him motivated mentally

We contacted his favourite football team, the team he supported, Aston Villa
They were very sympathetic to our needs and sent him memorabilia
He was surprised, so pleased to receive these gifts, you should see his face
We were so happy for him, to see him smiling, a smile you could embrace

He also had a get-well card, autographed by the players and a personal letter
He was invited to meet them when he was up and about, when he was better
That's what we wanted, something to look forward to, to give him motivation
All these things can only give him strength, to improve his current situation

He showed and told everyone, what he had received, you could see the pride
He loved showing off, he loved broadcasting, there's nothing he likes to hide
He felt special, he is, at least in our eyes, after all he is partially paralysed
This helped to ease the boredom, gave him variety and something to analyse

With this illness and the treatment, you have to get worse before you get better
That is fine with us, as long as the final conclusion becomes the latter
He was bedridden, on the nurses and his mum he was totally dependent
This was so difficult for him to accept mentally, after being so independent

It made him frustrated, giving rise to being bad-tempered and irritable
With all the medication, all what he is going through, it is understandable
On his mum and Caron his named nurse, he took out all his frustrations
She really had no choice, eventually he would apologise for his actions

The chemotherapy also made him very poorly, his appetite was still affected
All attempts and cajoling to make him eat solid food was firmly rejected

29

To maintain his blood cells, he had regular blood and platelet transfusion
His mental and physical strength was the key, he has a strong constitution

The treatment gave him high temperatures, at times he was so hot
It gave him the shivers, he was shaking, he is to go through such a lot
To see all these things happening to your child, is such a painful process
Yet we still have to be strong for his sake, we have to hide all this distress

Between the blocks of treatment, his powers of recovery were so remarkable
He would bounce back, he would start smiling again, once he was stable
He had another MRI scan to assess the impact of the first phase of treatment
It looked good, the tumours were shrinking, positive signs of improvement

His eating wasn't improving, he will soon need a gastric tube fitted,
said Mo the dietician
She wasn't popular with Aaron, because she tried to make him eat,
it was a war of attrition
Whenever she asked any questions, the reply was "Ask me mum,"
a new catchphrase
This was used very often, if he didn't want to answer,
he was going through another phase

The Treatment, The Second Phase

★

It was decided to transfer Aaron into a private vacant room on ward five
We are just thankful he has taken the treatment and has still survived
The reason for the move was because he is here for a long stay
We are just hoping he continues to progress, every day we pray

His lack of appetite was beginning to be a worry, although it was expected
Through his nose, painful for him, he has to have a gastric tube inserted
This means he will be fed liquid food intravenously during the night
It helps to retain his strength and stamina, although it is not a pretty sight

The first phase, the heavy chemo, has now been completed successfully
We feel elated, he is on the mend, but we know, we have to tread carefully
It is not over till it is over, that is the philosophy we have to maintain
Enjoy today, because as we all know, nothing in this life is ever certain

He starts his next course of treatment, we all feel a little more confident
Fingers crossed, legs crossed, he continues the same rate of improvement
The signs are looking good, the movement in his legs is slowly returning
He can gradually raise himself off the bed, it is all a new process of learning

The reduction of the tumours has slowly relieved the pressure on his nerves
That is why his movements are coming back, this is only what he deserves
After enduring so much already, this will give him hope and encouragement
Lift the cloud of despair, give him strength for the remainder of the treatment

We know for every high there is a low, it is painful to wee, he has an infection
The catheter has to be transferred directly into his bladder, another operation
He has become familiar with the theatre, so it is not a problem to him any more
He just takes it in his stride, sings a song as they push him through the door

31

He has overcome the operation, he is continuing to make rapid progress
Soon he is out of his bed into his wheelchair, independent, trying to impress
We were so happy when he made his first movement, now we are ecstatic
He is getting back to his cheerful self, but deep down we are still realistic

It is just another step along the road, another step towards being cured
We are still not counting our chickens, there is still more to be endured
He is having physiotherapy with Christine to build up his muscles again
He is over-keen, it is a slow process, we have to keep him under restrain

This is understandable considering he has been bedridden for so long
He wants his independence back, but we don't want anything to go wrong
We are hoping, someday soon, he will be able to go out in his wheelchair
He has been inside for four months, he needs to go outside for some fresh air

So far, so good, the second phase of treatment he has taken very well
But in life, you never know what is round the corner, you never can tell
His spirit has been high after months of gloom, at least he is going forward
Now he is more mobile, he is beginning to stamp his authority on the ward

He is going round in his wheelchair, introducing himself to the new patients
Aaron is nosey, he likes to know everyone, all the children and their parents
To all the little children on the ward, in some ways Aaron is acting like a godfather
He is always concerned for their well-being, he doesn't want them to suffer

Eventually, he was allowed to go out for the first time, one Sunday afternoon
He was so happy, he had a smile on his face, it couldn't come a moment too soon
His nurse Tonia suggested she could arrange a visit to the sea life centre
She phoned up, it was ok, just mention the hospital, it would be free to enter

It was a bright afternoon as we went down Birmingham's Broad Street
Aaron was so relieved to be out and about, although he wasn't on his feet
His first break from the hospital, hopefully, will do him the power of good
He could see the world outside again, boost his morale, it certainly should

We arrived at the sea life centre, the staff were aware, waiting to greet us
A photograph was taken, surrounded by the legs of a giant model octopus
We wandered through the centre looking at all the sea life that was there
He kept saying, "Excuse me please," so he could get by in his wheelchair

FEBURARY 1998

**AARON AND HIS DAD WITH A GIANT MODEL OCTOPUS
AT THE SEA LIFE CENTRE IN BIRMINGHAM**

THIS WAS HIS FIRST DAY OUT AFTER MONTHS OF BEING BEDRIDDEN

*All the people were so polite, gave him a smile, as we passed them by
They could see his disabilities, he couldn't walk, they could see why
Aaron was so inquisitive, making a mental note of all the varieties of fish
I was happy for him, if only things were different, that is my wish*

*He couldn't wait to get back to the hospital to tell them what he had seen
As soon as we got back on the ward, he couldn't stop talking, imagine the scene
A taste of freedom, a change of scenery, should help to give him motivation
Give him hope to pull him through this ordeal, to recover from this situation*

His improvement continues, he now has the ability to control his bladder

They remove the catheter, the tube, the bag is gone, he is now a lot happier
He has to vacate his room, another seriously ill patient needs the privacy
He has to move back to the main ward area, so all his friends he can see

So far Aaron's bravery, strength, in the face of adversity has amazed us all
He has taken his treatment, his disabilities, bounced back, still standing tall
His sense of humour has been acknowledged, we are all hoping he will recover
We know there is still more to come, another downer, we will soon discover

That came with another drug, which affected his eyes, they were so sore
He couldn't open them for three days, a feeling of blindness he has to endure
Initially he was scared, trying to overcome the effect the drug had produced
They gave him regular eye drops to counteract what the treatment had induced

Unable to open your eyes for a young lad, if only temporary, can be scary
You can't wait for it to return. How long will it take? You do become very wary
Yet Aaron accepted it, he was even seen doing dancing motions on his bed
He has become such a remarkable child, it was not surprising, let it be said

Once he could open his eyes again, he could continue his reading and writing
That is what he missed the most, it is what he loves, a true scholar in waiting
Unknown to us another surprise was coming our way, it came out of the blue
The BBC were filming a series, they wanted Aaron to be one of the chosen few

THE TREATMENT, THE SECOND PHASE

Aaron's case had come to Charlotte's (one of the BBC producers) attention
Apparently through the hospital grapevine, he has gained quite a reputation
She came to meet Aaron, they had quite an in-depth chat, to gain an insight
She was truly amazed by his attitude, it appeared to be love at first sight

Charlotte was so taken aback with our little man, after their conversation
She wanted to film Aaron's Story, obviously he had created an impression
His mum wasn't too keen, she is more reserved and dislikes all the attention
Dad is more like Aaron, more extrovert, but still she needs our permission

The bottom line, it was up to Aaron, he is sensible enough to make a decision
It could help him and if it was televised, to others it could be an inspiration
Aaron was approached, he was keen to be filmed, it would be his own story
His school friends could see him on TV, see him as a star, in all his glory

From now on the cameras became an integral part of Aaron's life in hospital
He was revelling in the limelight, it kept him interested, to us this was so vital
His hospital friends became part of his fan club, following him around
Wanting to be part of the scene, be an audience in the background

Another special event was due, his "swim up" to be a Cub Scout was imminent
The leaders wanted to do it in hospital, if they could get someone to consent
This wasn't a problem, the ward sisters were only too glad to help, to please
So it was arranged for a Sunday afternoon, when everyone would be at ease

Secretly Aaron asked Lyn the leader to bring a bunch of flowers for his mum
He knew he had given her a hard time over the months but she was still his chum
He used to blame her, saying it was her fault, he was in this predicament
His mum understood, she knew it was the drugs that affected his temperament

They brought the flag, with some of his friends from the pack for the ceremony
We dressed him in his uniform, took him down, there was so much harmony
We went through the "swim up" process, he did the sign and said his promise
He remembered the words, he came across so clearly, he came over so precise

THE TREATMENT, THE SECOND PHASE

He was now a fully-fledged Cub Scout, after a couple of years of being a Beaver
His ambition is to go camping under canvas, he couldn't wait, he was so eager
He will have to wait until he gets better, then his ambition will be realised
In the meantime, he can do his "first aid" badge, while being hospitalised

MARCH 1998

MARCH 1998 AARON DURING HIS "SWIM UP" CEREMONY FROM BEAVERS TO CUB SCOUT, WHILST IN HOSPITAL

He presented the flowers to his mum, she was taken aback, a little tearful
It was a surprise for her, but that is our son, so considerate, so thoughtful
Watching our son move from the Beavers to the Cub Scouts was so emotional
It was thinking back, that he has endured so much, to us it was so personal

AARON'S STORY IN VERSE

Another lumbar puncture for the drugs was now due, he needed to go to theatre
In the morning, Raquel came to get him prepared, he just totally ignored her
Trying to explain why she was there, while he was lying in bed reading a book
He was acting like the king of his domain, he wouldn't give her a second look

In her sweet Irish voice she asked him what time he went to bed last night
He was still being awkward, not showing any interest, not giving any respite
Eventually he said, "One o'clock", then he went into his "Ask mum" routine
So while he is asleep, she threatened to paint his legs in the Irish colour green

Eventually he went to theatre, he loved having the gas to
drift him off to dreamland
Fast asleep, not knowing what's going on, until he is awaken by the nurse's hand
The doctor remarked that Aaron was a right chatterbox,
wanting to know everything
Forever asking awkward questions, always wanting to know what was
happening

When you have answered him and you think to yourself,
don't ask me that question
What does he do, he goes and asks you that same question, that is our Aaron
Always putting doctors and nurses on the spot,
giving them a personal interrogation
They have to try and get it right, so he is satisfied, otherwise he
would go on and on

It is now time for another MRI scan to see if his improvement is ongoing
He doesn't like going into the tube, you have to keep perfectly still,
it is frightening
The scans came back. Dr Stevenson and Dr England came to tell him the result
"Hang on," said Aaron, "why can't I see it on the screen," acting like an adult

The two consultants knew Aaron very well,
so they felt obliged to grant him his wish
Although, it was a bit like sitting exams again, remarked Dr England
Looking at the scans, Dr Stevenson remarked, imagine your brain
was like a lollipop
The stick is your spinal column and your brain is the blob on the top

The tumours on his spine and on his brain have completely disappeared

Aaron didn't realise he had a brain tumour, we were so pleased it had cleared
At school he remembered being dizzy, probably caused by the tumour on the brain
Now the tumour has gone, maybe we can start planning for the future once again

With a question mark, the worst is over, he is now in a state of remission
He now needs to learn to walk again, he needs to continue his progression
We are now seeing some light, we are coming out of the tunnel of darkness
It's been a long haul, a traumatic period, it hasn't gone without some distress

Sometimes his gastric tube gave him problems, if he coughs it would come out
To reinsert it was an ordeal, he would be frantic, he would scream and shout
We would try to cajole him, talk to him, sometimes we had to hold him down
Once it was in, he realised it wasn't that bad, but he would still have his frown

He is now able to go out shopping locally, with his mum on a frequent basis
We give him treats, he deserves them after pulling through such a crisis
Aaron is looking well, the second phase of the treatment is coming to an end
The final phase, the maintenance blocks, the final one, we are left to contend

The Treatment, The Final Phase

⸺ ★ ⸺

This is the final phase of the protocol now that the tumours have gone away
He has to undergo a course of maintenance blocks to keep them at bay
Getting through this stage is vital, his chance of survival should increase
If we don't, his chances will be remote, he could be just another deceased

So we know we are not yet out of the woods, there is still some way to go
All we can do is keep carrying the load, live in hope, keep going to and fro
The best chance he had from the start was his age, he is at his strongest
He has done exceptionally well so far, the past few months have been the longest

We have meetings to discuss his future discharge, things need to be in motion
Our house, his school, needs to be assessed, to determine a plan of action
He is now classed as a child with special needs, because of his disabilities
We all know it could have been worse, we have to face life's harsh realities

It was nice to talk about Aaron going home, after six months of being hospitalised
The feeling of success, the feeling that we could be winning is difficult to realise
If he is up to it, we can take him home for a day, as part of his rehabilitation
Then for a weekend, suddenly, we are overcome by a feeling of elation

As always, Aaron was always kept informed of how things were progressing
Knowing he may go home soon was good news, at least it wasn't depressing
We now have something to look forward to, Aaron has an objective to achieve
The possibility of going home, getting back to normality, is so hard to believe

He still has to continue improving, he needs to start eating solids normally
For months all he has had is liquid food fed through his nose intravenously
Deena the care worker has gradually been coercing him to start eating

They even have a five pounds bet, an incentive, as long as there is no cheating

She is trying to tempt Aaron by giving him sausages, one of his favourite foods
She needs all her powers of persuasion, to convince him, it will do him good
He nibbles at it, complaining that he prefers his mother's Jamaican dinner
So Mum even starts bringing some from home, to see if she is on a winner

We can now start taking him home, he can once again see the world at large
This is the first stage, to see if we can cope, before he is finally discharged
He tells the nurses "I am off," the ward is so quiet, there is something missing
He tells them "I am back," the peace is broken, we know why, no need guessing

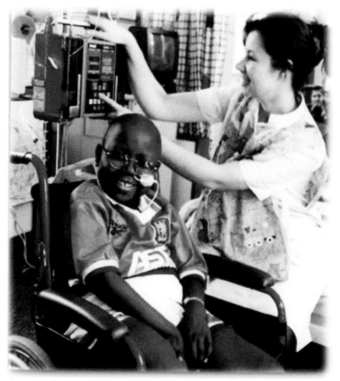

AARON DEMONSTRATING HIS BROAD SMILE
DRESSED IN HIS FAVOURITE PLAYER
AND TEAM FOOTBALL KIT
WHILE BEING NURSED BY ISOBEL

THE TREATMENT, THE FINAL PHASE

His outspoken views and forceful personality made him the boss of ward five
That is probably the main factor that has given him the strength to survive
So when the ward is peaceful, Aaron is either not around or he is sleeping
When he is discharged it won't be the same, but it is a memory worth keeping

All the children loved him, he was their leader, their source of inspiration
Even the parents grew close to him, his cheerful nature, his natural affection
They wanted to see him, although they may have returned with an infection
That is the magnetism he had, a long-stay patient with a natural attraction

The days at home have been successful, he is now ready to stop overnight
Mum has to learn how to prepare and set up his intravenous feed at night
We went home for the May Day bank holiday weekend and a family reunion
On Monday he could go to the open day at the new hospital, to get his opinion

It was a lovely weekend, we bought him a new game for his PlayStation
We invited his friends round on Sunday, to play this game full of action
On Monday, dad took him to the new hospital, to be filmed by the BBC
It was amazing, there was a massive queue, all waiting to look, to see

The cameras were there, as if they were waiting for the arrival of a star
The security guard separated the crowd, to allow me to park the car
They filmed us from the car park all through the hospital in his wheelchair
Aaron was in his element, he loves the limelight, the thought of being on air

He wheeled his way through the crowd, saying, "Excuse me please, thank you!"
They were only too pleased to let someone in a wheelchair pass on through
He went around the new wards, asking questions, seeing what he could find
He met some old friends, he was enjoying himself, with the cameras behind

His opinion of the hospital, it was nice, it was lovely, spacious and clean
He couldn't wait to move in with the other patients, wanting to be part of the scene
We would like to be home before the move, although he wanted to be there
He had set his heart on moving with his mates, up front in his wheelchair

We took him back that evening, he couldn't wait to talk about the new hospital
He kept going on and on to everyone, eventually it became a bit like a recital
We were all hoping now his discharge from the hospital is not too far away
Although for Aaron's sake, we don't mind if he is there for the transfer day

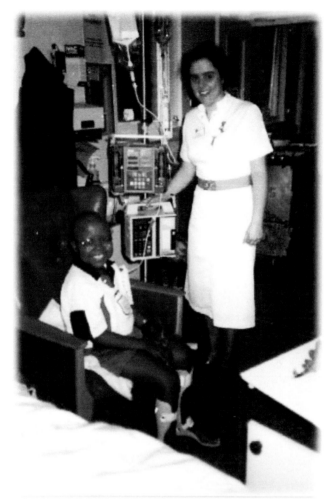

**AARON DRESSED IN HIS ENGLAND SHIRT
WITH JULIA
ONE OF HIS MANY FAVOURITE NURSES**

The Discharge

Aaron's recovery has been going so well, beyond our expectation
It is now time to review his case and examine the current situation
The aim is to discharge him from the hospital, as soon as possible
We could go home, if the facilities for home care are accessible

As parents we were so relieved, for the future we now have some hope
With his disabilities, the legacy left behind by his illness, we have to cope
We are just happy he is still here, after all the treatment he has endured
We will cope, of that there is no doubt, that is the one thing, that is assured

Before he can be discharged, there is much to learn regarding home care
Mum has to go through the learning process, what to do, how to prepare
His nightly feed, how to set it up, so he gets a constant feed during the night
What drugs to give him, when and how, take no chances, it all has to be right

A meeting was arranged by Dr Stevenson with all the specialists in attendance
This was essential to cover the necessary details, leaving nothing to chance
We discussed with the specialists the factors affecting Aaron's rehabilitation
It was important we all put our points across and had a proper consultation

He asked us if there were any problems when we took him home for the weekend
We coped quite well, we are confident, on his parents he can now depend
The conclusion was that he could be discharged and become an outpatient
He could finally go home, when he finishes his latest block of treatment

There was only one problem with discharging Aaron from the hospital
He would miss the transfer to the new hospital, to be part of it was vital
As Caron his named nurse explained, his mood would be one of devastation
The move has been his focal point for a while, he has done his investigation

He had even painted a welcome poster for the main door of ward fifteen
It was a picture of a rainbow, with bright colours, a vision he must have seen
To think he had been preparing all this, to miss the move by only a week
He won't want to go home, it would break his heart, a solution, we must seek

Although he might be back in hospital before the move with an infection
We must find a suitable alternative to overcome his possible dejection
It was suggested, we invite him to the ward for the transfer on Sunday
He could be filmed that day, to get his opinion, to hear what he had to say

The next stage was to bring Aaron to the meeting, to put him in the picture
He was already a bit upset, because he wasn't invited to discuss his future
He came in his wheelchair with all his drug lines, looking very observant
Realising the BBC cameras were filming the scenes, he was in his element

He was laid back as the consultant explained what the meeting was about
He could go home, be discharged from the hospital, he was being let out
You could see by his facial expression, he wasn't very happy, we know why
Missing the move, his main concern was on his mind, shown by his reply

The consultant then told Aaron if he was not in hospital for the transfer
He could come down on the day, to be one of the first visitors there
He could still feel part of the move and see his friends in the new place
We were all a bit more relieved, as a little smile appeared on his face

Now that he knows he could feel part of the move, he was more bearable
If it wasn't possible, his temperament, his mood, would have been unthinkable
The last week of his treatment in hospital seemed so slow, seemed so long
We couldn't wait for Monday, back home, we are hoping nothing goes wrong

The day we have to leave the hospital has arrived at last, it is now here
We are happy and sad, mixed emotions, we have spent so much time in there
The daily routine of the hospital, has been our way of life for almost a year
We now have to readapt to our home life; it won't be normal, that is our fear

The physiotherapist Christine came to see him to go through the exercises
He needs to continue them at home, to overcome the effects of his paralysis
As usual Aaron was reading a book, not interested in what she was trying to say
Christine said, "You are not listening to me, are you?" as she took the book away

Aaron said, "I can read and listen at the same time when someone is talking"
"Even I can't do that," insisted Christine, she knows Aaron can be frustrating
Eventually, Aaron relented, they did their final exercise walk with his rollator
Christine giving her final instructions, as they went up and down the corridor

Christine has grown quite fond of the little man. According to Aaron,
"She is all right"
She is happy and sad: happy he is going home, sad because he will be out of sight
They have developed a special bond, they have spent so much time together
Deep down in her heart, we believe she will miss Aaron, the little terror

All this episode was being filmed by the cameras, so after she had gone
What does Aaron say, "No more questions, I am reading, leave me alone"
Then his least favourite person, Mo the dietician, made an appearance
A typical Aaron statement, "Oh! Not you again!" with a typical glance

He just blanked her out, because she still wanted him to try to eat
Hopefully when he gets home, he will succumb to his mum's Jamaican treat
Finally Donella the ward manager came to finalise his visit on Sunday
She promised he will be one of the first visitors, it will be such a happy day

It is now time to leave, we must keep our positive attitude, as we have before
We have been to hell and back, suffered nightmares, can we take any more?
We pack all his gear. It is like moving home, there is so much he has acquired
Aaron said, "He was the king of ward five," now he is going, he has been fired

As we made our way down the corridor, Julia asked Aaron for a goodbye kiss
As usual Aaron said, "No" as she leaned forward, she was standing next to Trish
"Oh, all right then," he said, so she gave him a cuddle and a kiss on the cheek
Trish said, "I want good reports from your mum, we will be seeing you next week"

The TV cameras were there to film our final goodbyes to the staff and our friends
Filming Aaron has been an experience to remember, now it is coming to an end
They filmed us from the ward to the car, with tears, laughter, hugs and kisses
All rolled into one, all emotions surfacing, all with good luck and best wishes

Home At Last

---★---

The drive home was enjoyable, such a sense of relief to be going home at last
Hoping, praying, the previous six months are gone forever, it's in the past
From experience, we can't afford to be complacent, it's not over till it's over
There is still more treatment to undergo, still a lot more ground to cover

Now we are home at last, the neighbours are glad to see him, our little man
Hugs and kisses from our neighbour Margie, she loves him dearly, as only she can
It is nice to be home, in your own surroundings, to be a family together again
It will be just nice to relax, sleep in your own bed, trying to relieve the strain

Aaron settled back into his home life, although he is no longer independent
Being partially disabled, on his mum and dad he is now so dependent
Obviously he still tries to help himself, that is his character, that's his style
His strength of mind has kept him going, let's hope it stays for a long while

He has to continue his lessons. His home tutor, Mrs Douglas, he has to greet
She had heard so much about Aaron, the little man she can't wait to meet
It didn't take long before they were on the same wavelength, talking away
That is typical of Aaron, so inquisitive, still cheeky, still having a lot to say

He still had to go back to the new hospital once a week, as an outpatient
To test his blood count, he still needs two blocks of the maintenance treatment
On the first visit Dr Stevenson was expecting Charlotte and the cameras to be in tow
Not surprising, when considering they have been following him for some time now

He couldn't wait to be a patient in the new hospital, blood count permitted
He was upset when his count wasn't right and he couldn't be admitted
He had to explain to him that this is a hospital, it is not a hotel
Aaron didn't care, he just wanted to experience the new ward, you can tell

He was invited back to his school for a day out to the museum with his class
He was so happy to return, to see his mates again, we couldn't let it pass
Parents, teachers, his classmates were so glad to see him back at school
Typical of Aaron, he took it in stride, so laid back, acting as Mister Cool

We escorted him onto the coach, hoping he will cope and enjoy his day out
Although we were a little concerned, really we had nothing to worry about
Mum spent the day thinking of her little man, wondering how he is getting on
I suppose it is typical motherhood, they have been so close, it is her only son

We went to fetch him, he had enjoyed his day, it's part of his rehabilitation
We were happy for him, he is on his way back, he's started his integration
This is all part of the process of getting a life, getting back to some normality
It was the first stage in overcoming and being able to cope with his disability

We took him to see his old teachers at the infant school next door
They welcomed him, they were so happy to see him out and about once more
He had spent three wonderful years there, he was popular, a success
In their eyes they were trying to hold back the tears, the tears of happiness

It was an eventful day, one, at times we thought we would never discover
But it has happened, he is on his way to recovery, the first hurdle is now over
We try to make the most of his time at home, Mum has got back into a routine
Doing the shopping, doing his feed at night and ensuring he takes his medicine

The Visit To The New Hospital

✦

On Sunday we went to the new hospital, as promised by the consultant
We drove into the car park, Aaron spotted the cameras in an instant
Asking "Where are the patients?" as he was hanging out the car window
He clambered out all eager and keen, talking away, his face all aglow

The first person he saw was Dr Stevenson; he was glad to see him once again
As usual he took time out to welcome Aaron, have a chat in sunshine, not rain
The cameras followed us to the new ward, which was now number fifteen
He couldn't wait to meet his friends and the nurses, he was really keen

His first concern was for baby James, his adopted hospital brother
He had to give him a cuddle, a wonderful sight, seeing them together
Then it was off to see his mate Jadon, the new king, who had something to say
He was talking to him, his brothers and parents, in that old, familiar way

He was soon asking questions about the new facilities on his exploration
With Trish the Sister, the unfortunate one who has to give an explanation
He wanted to test out the new mod cons, what each button was used for
It was what was expected of Aaron, after all, he hasn't been here before

He was interviewed, explaining what it's like to be home after so long away
He was seen chatting away, perhaps saying things, he shouldn't really say
Like going up and down the stairs, on his own, proving he was very bold
He was supposed to be careful, but that's him, not doing what he was told

So he said, "I am a careful boy, aren't I," he was trying to be independent
He is his own man, as we all know, he has always been very confident

As usual he was telling all, with that well-known, cheeky smile on his face
A smile so broad, with a twinkle in his eyes, he brightened up the place

He was happy, because he was one of the first visitors to the new hospital
His dream has been fulfilled, to be there on the day of the move was so vital
We can now go home in peace, so he can continue on the road to recovery
He has been there, seen it, he has completed his mini voyage of discovery

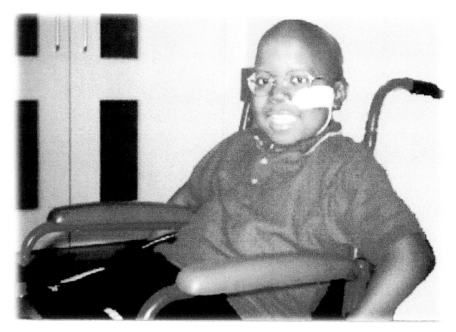

AARON VISIT TO THE NEW HOSPITAL, MADE HIM HAPPY, BECAUSE HE WAS ONE OF THE FIRST VISITORS.

Home At Last

After the visit, Mum is trying hard to encourage him to eat her home cooking
He is still resisting, the drugs are still affecting his appetite, he is just looking
We hope in time his body will be free from drugs, his appetite will return
We just need to be patient, keep up the encouragement, not to be too concerned

He is continuing his lessons with his home tutor, a new friend he has found
She has grown quite fond of him and always looks forward to coming around
A rapport has developed that makes teaching him an enjoyable experience
She is amazed by the astuteness of his mind and his undoubted intelligence

He has another appointment at the hospital, once again to have a blood test
He still can't wait to be admitted onto the new ward, he is doing his level best
The Macmillan nurse Cheron came in with us to see the doctor on this occasion
As usual, he showed his cheekiness and told her off,
for interrupting his conversation

The results came through, his blood count is fine, at last he can come back in
He shouts "Yes! Yes! I am coming back" everyone could hear, it was amazing
Most people want to get out, yet he wants to come in, it didn't seem right
That is Aaron, he is so different, so unpredictable, so completely forthright

At last he was back in the ward with his mates, he has achieved his ambition
The treatment will take a couple of days, unless he gets an adverse reaction
So here he was again back in hospital, with drips attached to his central line
We are hoping he is problem-free and after the couple of days he will be fine

After a day or so, the novelty of being in the new hospital began to wear thin
He wanted to go back home, the new ward wasn't like the old one, it was boring
The old one had a unique atmosphere, because we were like sardines in a tin
The new one is more spacious, more segregated, the closeness is missing

Aaron also had new nurses to contend with, which didn't please him at all
He was used to the old ones, they were used to his mannerisms and his call
Luckily the treatment went well, no reactions, he came back out on Saturday
At least he has been in, he has got it out of his system, nothing more to say

Back at home, we try to give him plenty of variety, to reduce the boredom
We know he is restricted by his disability, but at least he has got his freedom

His friends come round to play, they have supported him through thick and thin
It is so important to us, to him, to his morale, to give him this wanted feeling

We take him shopping, it is so different now with him being in a wheelchair
It's like going on an expedition, you sometimes think life just isn't fair
But we have to make the most of what we have got, this is so important
It could have been a lot worse, he is here with us, this is so significant

He likes going shopping, he wheels himself around, seeing what's on display
He always wants us to buy him something, always wanting us to make his day
He is still attracted to people we meet, his charisma hasn't gone, it is still there
So he is chatting away, still an extrovert, although he is now in a wheelchair

At home he enjoys painting pictures and writing stories on his computer
He likes to demonstrate his expertise to Mrs Douglas, his home tutor
A special needs assessor arrives to see him, to test his mental aptitude
They have a discussion, he is amazed and also surprised by his attitude

He has never been so far in the book, he can't believe he is only eight
His mental age is beyond his years, his reading and aptitude is first-rate
We were not really surprised: he has proved time and again he is clever
That has been seen over the last year, now it's shown more than ever

Dad has a week off work, to have a rest, to be home with his family
We also had to go and fetch his sister back home from university
Her first year at university is over, she has completed her examinations
She is coming home for the summer, to be with us and for some relaxation

Due to being ill, Aaron and his mum have never been to where his sister was staying
The journey this time was happier, although it was like going back to the beginning
Aaron wanted to see the hall of residence, you could see he was getting excited
At last we are together again, out of the hospital, a family of four reunited

Aaron can't wait to see her room, to see if it is like the one at home – a mess
Surprise! Surprise! Nothing changes, you know the outcome, no need to guess
Anyway, we tidy her room and pack her things in the car, close the door
Another episode is over, the drive home is a lot more pleasant than before

At home, we are feeling more relaxed, we have waited so long for this day
At one point we doubted if it would ever come, now it is here, hopefully to stay

His sister finds herself a summer job, to raise funds to continue her degree
She can also take time out to unwind, for three months, at last she is free

At least, that is what we hoped, it all depends on Aaron overcoming his illness
He has come this far, the signs are still good, he is not showing any distress
We know with this disease it will be years before you can feel comfortable
But he still needs to get through the maintenance treatment, when he is able

His Auntie Pat decided to give us a break, she will take him out for a day
That was a good idea, he could go visiting his relatives and have a play
He went round to his Uncle Bobby's, played on his computer and the internet
That gave him a thrilling new experience, one to remember, not to forget

He went to see Grandma, Auntie Novlet, to them he was looking cured
They were all pleased to see him out and about, after what he had endured
After months in hospital an innocent little man, who hasn't committed any sins
It brought tears of joy to Grandma, just watching him play with his cousins

It was a moment, she may have thought she would never see again
All her grandchildren around her, playing with her grandson, free from pain
If you can picture the scene, you can appreciate, why she shed tears of joy
He has been to hell and back, although, he is a little man, he is still her little boy

He came back home full of beans, another step along the road, another success
We can't believe how he is improving, we are hoping he continues his progress
At this rate he will be walking again and in September he will back at school
But we mustn't jump to any conclusions from experience, it is the golden rule

His Auntie Kath wanted to take him to the cinema, she is also his godmother
This gives mum a break, gives him a bit of variety, as they went off together
Kath was glad to take him, to have a laugh with him, helping us to relieve the strain
Aaron loved it; this is all part of getting him back to a normal life again

We had a phone call from his school, Aaron was invited back on Friday
He was specially invited to watch his class performance of a Roman play
We took him there, someone was missing, they gave him a few lines to say
In front of the pupils and teachers, he said his lines, Oh, what a happy day!

His classmates welcomed him back into the fold, he was looking so sound
He had a maths lesson, he played his part, they took him into the playground

He played as best he could, he joined in, although he was wheelchair-bound
As usual he had a lot to say, for him, it was great, he had broken new ground

Mrs Douglas brought him home, from his broad smile, he had enjoyed his day
As parents, we were so happy for our son, he is recovering, he's on his way
On Sunday afternoon, his mum took him over to see his Nanny and Granddad
He started complaining of headaches, once again we are hoping it isn't too bad

A-B-C

Found on Aaron's computer after his passing.

The Relapse

We gave him some medicine, hoping that will ease the pain
Praying that is all he needs, we don't want to travel this road again
Our happiness could be short-lived, it could be another sad weekend
We were worried for our little man, will this nightmare ever end?

The headaches got worse, he was back in hospital Monday night
We were trying to be calm, in this dark tunnel, is there no light?
He was admitted for more tests and yet another brain scan
Our emotions were in turmoil, we prayed for our little man

We feared the worst, as they gave him more drugs to ease the pain
Is he relapsing? Is he OK? Or are we going down this road once again?
By Friday the results had come through; is it what we had feared?
We held hands tightly, as the doctors said sorry, it has reappeared

We were overcome, inconsolable, the tears flowed from me and my wife
Are we coming to the end? The final chapter in this, our son's short life
In the time span of a week, we have gone from elation, much happiness
To the depths of despair, deflation, our hearts filled with much sadness

The doctors, nurses tried to comfort us, give us some reassurance
We were oblivious to their comforting words, we were in a trance
We composed ourselves, and realised, where there is life, there is hope
After a nine-month nightmare, will we still have the strength to cope?

As always, the next stage was to see and explain to our little man
What would be his reaction, the normal way, as only Aaron can
The consultant said sorry, then explained in detail the latest situation
As usual at the end, Aaron said, "Excuse me, can I ask a question?"

More tests were necessary to obtain a final confirmation
More experts to be consulted, to plan a course of action
He needed another MRI scan, we had to go by ambulance
It was necessary to be more conclusive, is there a chance?

The ambulancemen were tremendous they waited for us
I explained to them his problem, they knew it was serious
A few days passed by, before the results came through
The tumours were showing on his spine, I guess we knew

We were told the chances of survival are extremely slim
We needed a miracle, all we could do is pray for him
We hoped to still fulfil his dream and take him to France
Don't give up, put things in place, there may be a chance

A new course of steroids and radiotherapy was the only hope
For a better quality life, a chance to live, how long is the rope?
Maybe weeks, months, if we are lucky it could be years
We just don't know, we are helpless, but we have our fears

Once again, our little man was told, what was to be done
Hoping he would be positive, find the strength to carry on
In our hearts we knew, in his inner self, he felt defeated
In a quiet moment he told us, it wouldn't be completed

Aaron was still the same, during this period on the ward
Telling everyone his little secrets, still so very forward
Watching the World Cup, supporting England till the end
Concerned for baby James, Victoria and Jadon, his friends

He contracted shingles and blamed one of his best mates
He went into a high-dependency unit, to await his fate
With people he had upset, his conscience he made clear
As if deep down in his heart, he knew the end was near

The tumour on his brain was affecting him mentally
You could see his memory was going slowly
It was so sad to see his main strength disappearing
Struggling to comprehend as if he was hard of hearing

You mentally start reliving, what has happened to us
Like him dreaming of his granddad last Christmas
We thought then, he might be having a premonition
We have kept quiet since, too frightened to mention

Now it is possible, that terrible dream may come true
We still don't want to believe it, he will see it through
Our last hope rests in the form of this new treatment
We must remain positive, we know it is not very pleasant

They commenced the new treatment on Friday evening
Our concerns are growing, but still we must keep believing
That the beginning of the end will be only a bad dream
He will still be with us, things are not what they seem

The Beginning of The End

The initial signs were he was slow to respond to the new treatment
Just looking tired, not thinking straight, not even making a comment
He perked up after a few days, he was back to himself, back on form
Making cheeky statements, talkative, as usual not wishing to conform

He received a present, the new World Cup 98 game for his PlayStation
He was allowed to come home, to rest, before the next course of action
We were so happy to have him home for a while, free from any pain
Little did we know it was the last time, he wouldn't be coming home again

That evening he watched the television, he and his sister played the game
Shouting, laughing and winning as usual, things appeared the same
Mum tucked him into bed and gave him a hug and a goodnight kiss
He remarked, "It's lovely to be at home, in my own bed," it was bliss

The next morning, when he awoke, his speech was slurred
Complaining of headaches, overnight, it has all reoccurred
It all happened so quickly, for him, we were trying not to cry
In the back of our minds, is this the final chapter? Is he going to die?

Is it the beginning of the end, as he said, "Mum, I don't like this"
"You will be OK," with tear-filled eyes, she gave him a cuddle and a kiss
Nothing improved, we took him back to hospital in the afternoon
Overnight it has come back so suddenly, "Oh no!" it seems too soon

Doctor, what can you do? Is it out of control? It's so aggressive
Is there anything you can do? Please try and make it regressive
These were our thoughts as they did more tests and an examination
Hoping, hoping and praying they could raise our expectation

Clutching at straws, there was one final thing that could be done
This was to give him a course of the steroid dexamethasone

If he didn't respond to this, we could be facing the final curtain
A day later, still no improvement, now death almost seems certain

We were then told, the next twenty-four hours would be crucial
To survive, there needs to be some positive signs, it was essential
On Saturday, he had a fit, the pressure was increasing on his brain
We thought it was the end, although he didn't seem to be in pain

He eventually came out of the fit, relieved, it was another false alarm
He seemed as well as to be expected, he hadn't come to any real harm
Asking the doctor, is she going to give him something to make him better
Those were desperately sad words, a cry for help, sooner rather than later

The doctor said, "I need to talk to your mum and dad in a quiet place"
There is nothing more we can do, as the tears streamed down our faces
It is the beginning of the end, how long? It is impossible to be accurate
Hours, days, weeks, we will make it painless, finally we knew his fate

We were all devastated, knowing our little man is slipping away
We cuddled him, talked to him, for a miracle we would still pray
Yet in his semi-conscious state he still tried to talk and write
We couldn't understand him, although he still had some fight

He asked for his pencil and pad, did his six-times table in a neat line
Then strangely, it may seem, he wrote 9999
We tried to work out what he meant, we tried to find an interpretation
We didn't have an answer, a scholar to the end, keeping up his education

Nellie, Ron and Lou came to see us a couple of days before the end
Trying to hold back the tears, they realised they were losing a friend
In the corridor outside his room, we explained his current condition
In their faces you could see they felt for us, in our present situation

Eventually he was connected to a morphine drip to ease the pain
We were reluctant, afraid to leave him, it was a tremendous strain
We had to be there until the very end, for when the final curtain came down
We would never forgive ourselves, if we weren't there for him, weren't around

Once again he asked for his pencil and pad, with his fading breath
His life was slowly ebbing away, you could see, he was close to death

He found the strength to write the word "enjoy" twice, a word so significant
In the circumstances, that current climate, that word became so poignant

FLAG OF JAMAICA

Aaron was fascinated by the world. Found this on the computer after his passing.

**AARON'S FINAL WRITTEN WORD, "ENJOY",
HIS SIX-TIMES TABLE AND 9999**

It struck a chord, we were so sorry it wasn't spoken, it wasn't heard
That was to become his final written message, his final written word
He may be telling us to try to enjoy our life, without him, our little man
Which is going to be so hard, but we must try for his sake, the best we can

He was now making a gurgling noise, which is known as the death rattle
This is a sure sign, that after fighting for so long, he has lost the battle
We have to use a suction tube to remove the mucus from his throat
You have this sinking feeling, the end is near, you are no longer afloat

On Monday he awoke early and for an hour he had his final say
We couldn't understand him, we were so sorry, Oh! What a sad day!
He fell asleep, his chest heaving up and down, breathing heavily
As the day passed, he started to deteriorate, he was going steadily

Suddenly his mum cried out, "Oh my baby," and after a few false alarms
We tried to turn him, his breathing stopped, he died in our arms
The tears flowed, we hugged him, our little man has finally gone
On his last breath, the sun came out to shine, oh how it shone!

With the sunshine, a rainbow appeared, to brighten up the sky
A fitting end to the one who was so colourful, an appropriate goodbye
This feeling you have inside is so difficult to understand, to explain
All you know, it really hurts to lose the one you love, all you feel is pain

Once we finally knew his fate, we didn't want him to linger on
In an unconscious state, unable to talk, it wouldn't be fair to Aaron
Knowing your only son is dying and there is nothing that you can do
Is such a horrendous situation, that no parents should to go through

It has taken three weeks to the day from relapse to when he passed away
It has taken three days from his cry for help, to this terrible, sad day
For this we are thankful for, the strain would have been too unbearable
Sitting and watching him fade away, is something that is unforgettable

Now our family, nurses, children's parents cried, sharing our grief
With Aaron lying there asleep, his time in this world seemed so brief
His mum and his auntie gave him a bed bath, to make him clean
He was dressed in his England kit, he is asleep, looking so serene

It seems appropriate, he was patriotic, for him England were the cream
He was planning for the next World Cup in 2002 with the England team
He died the day after the World Cup final, although we told him who had won
We don't know if he understood us, so sad he won't be here for the next one

AARON PLANNING FOR 2002 WORLD CUP.
SADLY, HE WASN'T HERE TO SEE IT.

Now among our family, friends, an aura of silence and sorrow prevailed
Has the treatment, the parents tender, loving care, has it really failed?
The answer was yes, he was given everything possible, it wasn't enough
He fought his best fight till the end, gave it his best shot, he was tough

After all the punishing treatment he has taken, he deserved to survive
We felt so sorry for him, he showed so much courage in trying to stay alive
So why him? Why has he been taken from us? Why does it have to be our Aaron?
Maybe one day we will know why he is in heaven? Why he is the chosen one?

For now all we can do is comfort each other, as they take him away
To the mortuary he will be going, for just a temporary stay

Mum, dad and sister went to see him all alone, we just cried
We touched him, talked to him, caressed him and said goodbye

We were so sad going home, leaving our only son behind
Our family minus one, thinking life is so cruel, so unkind
We arrived home feeling drained and completely lifeless
It seemed we were in a trance, no talking, so much sadness

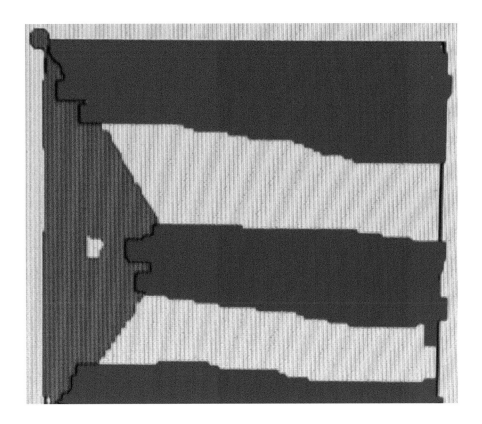

FLAG OF CUBA

Aaron was fascinated by the world. Found this
on the computer after his passing.

The Funeral

We just could not believe how things have changed so quickly
We have gone from relapse to death, in three weeks, exactly
We were planning for the future, while he was in remission
Now God has taken him, he must have completed his mission

Now here we are, making the final arrangements for his funeral
It had to be special, after all, he was unique, he was the General
It is so hard to believe, you are arranging your son's internment
This is not right, he is too young, it should be one of us, his parent

We had to carry on, running on adrenaline, this does not seem real
We had to go through the process, regardless of how we really feel
We visited the funeral directors with the necessary documentation
They were patient and understanding, they showed so much compassion

I had to write his tribute, from birth to death, covering all of his years
I was inspired by him, it was easy, the words just flowed, I was in tears
I believe the final result was a reflection of Aaron through and through
I gave it to his mum to read, that's lovely she said! Aaron, it's just you

We thought of Aaron, trying to imagine how he would want to go out
It needed to be a celebration of his life, that there was no doubt
The music had to be his favourites, showing sadness and happiness
It had to be modern, after all he was young with a carefree freshness

The entrance music, a classical mood, 'Pavane' the BBC World Cup theme
After all, he was watching it till the end, following the England team
In the middle of the service, after the tribute, would be "Missing you"
A sad song, the last tape in his Walkman, the one he was rocking to

The final piece of music, an upbeat reggae song called "One love"
This reflected him, where he is coming from, where he is going, above
In the words, there is no hiding place from the father of creation
This was perfect, because the singer was also asking a question

We went to see the location of his grave, it was ideal, on a hill
You could think he's looking down, so peaceful, so tranquil
We had to decide what clothes he should wear on his final day
It was to be his Aston Villa football kit, it was perfect in every way

The day before the funeral we went to see him in the chapel of rest
He was in his little coffin, looking beautiful, looking his very best
Once again we were overcome with tears, feeling so sad, so sad
Why did we have to lose him, someone we love, someone we had

Thinking life is just not fair, we shouldn't have to go through this ordeal
It is all a dream, he will suddenly wake up with a smile, it's not real
We eventually had to leave our little man behind, to get back to reality
Now we are back in the real world, we must be strong to keep our sanity

During the week, family, friends and neighbours came to pay their respects
We had over a hundred cards, some with tributes, which we didn't expect
They gave us strength to know, he was such a popular child, to so many
That he didn't die in vain, he left his impression and we know he was funny

Now the night before his final day on this God's earth has arrived at last
You cannot sleep, you're tired, your mind is awake, thinking of the past
The next day ahead is daunting, you are trying to believe, it is not true
You are trying to summon strength from somewhere, to see you through

In no time at all floral tributes are being delivered, covering the drive
Cars are coming, family, relations and friends are beginning to arrive
Some you haven't seen for years, all in sombre dress, all sharing your loss
All grieving for you, saying sorry, it is understandable, he was the boss

The floral tributes are a reflection of his life, a football and an open book
A globe embedded in flowers, he loved the world, they all came to look
All these flower arrangements tell a story of our little man, our Aaron
It is him in his living life, that is their memory of him, now he has gone

The hearse, funeral cars are now coming, driven by men dressed in black
They come to a halt, our son with a floral heart on his coffin in the back
Tears are flowing from sad faces, his mum crying; Oh Aaron, oh Aaron
Why did you have to go? Why did you have to leave us? Oh why? My son

The funeral procession of cars is now on its way moving so slow, so slow
We are all feeling deflated, all feeling so sad, all feeling so low, so low
We arrive at the church, people with solemn faces, gathering all around
All in mourning, all waiting so peacefully, you couldn't hear a sound

His uncles are the pallbearers, carrying his little coffin, it is such a sad day
We are following behind, supporting each other, our son leading the way
The church is full, so many people have come to say their last goodbyes
It is Aaron's day, they are here to show their respect, that's why

The BBC World Cup theme 'Pavane' starts playing, as we made our entrance
The mourners are so quiet, not a whisper, they remain in complete silence
The vicar says his introductory speech, explaining why we are here
It is to be a celebration of his short life, this he made very clear

Hymns were sung, prayers read, they listened to words from the Bible
His dad read his tribute, although emotional, he was clear and audible
This was the sad part of the service, especially with the song "Missing you"
It was hard to have dry eyes, they could see Aaron through and through

The service ended on an uplifting note, with the happy song "One love"
It was the perfect ending, he has gone to the father of creation up above
It is now the time to remove his coffin, to take him to his final resting place
To the cemetery we went, a procession of cars, all going at a very slow pace

At his burial plot, his dad's desire was to lower his only son into the ground
He carried him to the grave with his three uncles, the inner strength he found
We held the ropes and slowly lowered him down to rest, into his eternal bed
People were gathered all around, heads bowed as the final prayers were said

We threw soil and red roses into his grave, whispered our final goodbyes
This was to be the saddest, most tearful moment, you can't help but cry
We started to fill in his grave, the traditional Jamaican way with our funerals
Where relatives and friends bury their own, in this case our little General

We filled in his grave and formed a mound, covered completely with flowers
In some ways it was a sad but beautiful sight seeing such a variety of colours
His globe was buried with him, he has gone to a new world, one to explore
The burial is now over, our son is resting in peace, the son so many adore

The cortège slowly returns to the church hall for the post-funeral reception
Refreshments are laid on, this is essential to continue the celebration
Guests are from near and far, neighbours, hospital staff, teachers, the BBC
Representatives from work, from his Cub Scouts, he was so popular, you see

We mingle with the mourners, thank them for coming to share, this, our sad day
There were many who attended the service, nothing would have kept them away
They all thought we as a family did our little man proud, the service was Aaron
We felt a sense of relief, it went so well, the sad part, we wish he hadn't gone

Little groups of people were discussing Aaron, reliving and sharing stories
You could see from the smiles on their faces, they have many happy memories
This is how we wish to remember our son, someone who brought joy to all
Someone who wasn't anonymous, but someone in the future, you can recall

The guests are now slowly departing, to continue their life, their own way
We can only hope, they have all retained something from this memorable day
We thank the helpers for preparing such a wonderful spread for our guests
They did us proud, they were volunteers, they were brilliant, the very best

Now we have to return to our empty house, our close family are here with us
We discuss our little man, how to cope without him, life must have a purpose
They have to go, we know they will support us through the grieving process
The saddest day of our life is now over, all that's left is a feeling of emptiness

Our Little Man, Aaron (Eulogy)

⸺ ✪ ⸺

This is a tribute to our little man, Aaron Nathan Senior, from his family
We were privileged to have him with us for eight years and eight months

On the twentieth of November 1989, our wish was granted
A baby boy, born from love, what we always wanted
He popped out, his cries greeted the world
A family of four complete, one boy, one girl

A typical baby boy, he could not rest
Until he received the comfort of his mother's breast
Within days, he turned yellow, jaundice appeared
He spent ten days gathering a tan, before it cleared

His magnetism became evident to strangers, as a toddler
Which never diminished as he got older
With a cheeky smile and infectious laughter
Attracting mothers, fathers, sons and daughters

At school, he was an exceptional child, we were surprised
As parents we were perhaps naïve, we never realised
His thirst for knowledge we must mention
Always reading, writing and asking a question

His constant talking got him into trouble at school
With his knowledge and intelligence, he was nobody's fool
He was a Cub Scout and a little Beaver
Always keen to learn, always eager

In his lifetime Aaron was not his only name
He was "Mr Know-it-all", "Chatterbox", to children it's just a game
With his knowledge, "The Professor" also became his title
It was just amazing, considering he was so little

In the last year of his life, he touched the hearts of many
Cracking jokes, cheeky comments, so humorous, oh so funny
At times he was a little genius, a wise man, oh so serious
Leaving an everlasting impression, to us so special, so precious

He was the boss of ward five, an upfront kind of guy
Always debating, arguing with doctors, nurses, asking why? Why?
An inspiration, a shining light, to children, parents, and so kind
He set the scene, led from the front, never from behind

He had the operations, the drugs, endured the pain
He took it in his stride, bouncing back again and again
Causing havoc around the ward in his personalised "R reg" wheelchair
In the distance all you see is the top of his head, with no hair

With Aaron "what you see is what you got"
A strong character with charisma, a fighter, always saying a lot
To us, it seems, he has lived his life, with no fears
His attitude, knowledge, experiences, defying his tender years

Remember we have all learnt so much from Aaron
We are so proud to have had him, as a brother and a son
In his short lifetime, he was in the limelight, a star
It is so hard to believe, he has travelled so far

In his short life he was our little man, not a little boy
He was writing to the end, his last word was "enjoy"
That tells its own story, his spirit will live on and on
Hold the treasured memories, he hasn't really gone

I know in his heart, he wants us to be happy, not sad
He's gone to heaven to be with his granddad
Now Aaron listen to me your dad, we will shed some tears
Try to enjoy our life, until we meet again, in the future years

Aaron, the twinkle in your eye, your smile, will never die
You gave love and received love
Always, always love you, from Mum, Dad and Theresa

AARON WITH BIG GRANDMA
AT HIS CHRISTENING

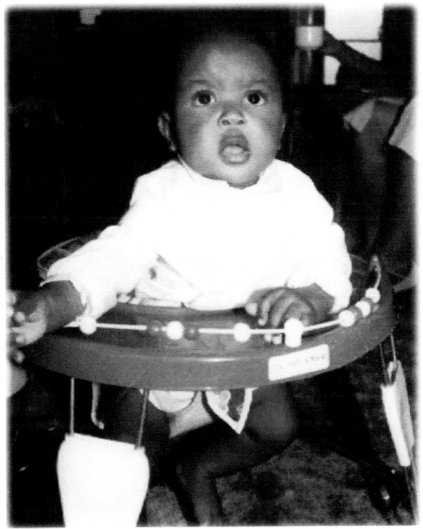

**AARON LEARNING
TO WALK CAUSING HAVOC AROUND
THE HOUSE IN HIS BABY WALKER**

AARON THE TODDLER PLAYING IN THE SNOW

AARON THE PROUD SCHOOLBOY

Tributes And Donations

★

We decided it would be mainly family flowers, a good cause for all donations
It would be to the Children's Hospital and to cancer research foundations
We believe other people especially children should benefit from Aaron
Knowing him our son, it would have been his wish, now that he has gone

Since our son's death we have had over a hundred cards and messages
Some came from people who hardly knew him, from people of all ages
It was heartwarming and also sad for us, but they gave us great comfort
Just to know there are so many people out there, giving us their support

The tributes praised our son, recalling special moments in the past
Some were short, some were long, it is clear these moments will last
Most gave the same message that our little man had a true uniqueness
They congratulated him on his bravery, his fighting spirit, his kindness

Some said they would have loved to have followed, his development
He would have made his mark in the world, what a compliment
We read these tributes over and over, they will stay with us forever
We will put them in a special place, to read in the future or whenever

The donations were over a thousand pounds, this shows his pulling power
We shared it out, the majority to the oncology ward to buy a blood warmer
This is where he spent most of his time in hospital, where he was famous
It will have a plaque engraved with his name, he will never be anonymous

Edwards House had a share, a home for families who need to live away
This would have pleased Aaron that is where his hospital friends had to stay
The general Children's Hospital fund and cancer research had what remained
It is nice to know that Aaron didn't die in vain, so many people have gained

Aaron would have been pleased to know that the money was shared out

That is his nature, a child of variety, never boring, that's what he was about
It was an ordeal going back to the hospital to give out the cheques personally
Although it brought back so many sad memories, but we had to do it formally

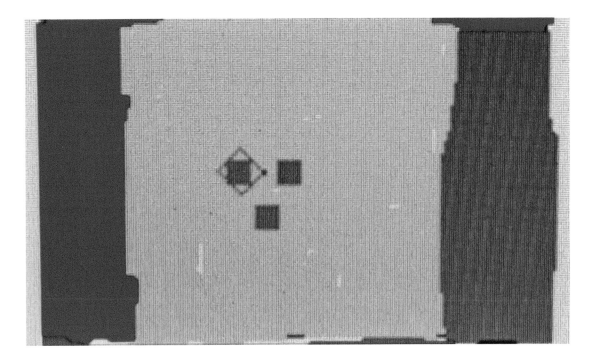

FLAG OF SAINT VINCENT AND THE GRENADINES

Aaron was fascinated by the world. Found on the computer after his passing.

Feeling of Emptiness

He has been laid to rest, underneath a cascade of flowers
Floral tributes reflect his life, many varieties, many colours
Tears are falling, as you recall, his happy smiling face
Deep in our hearts, we believe he has gone to a better place

Friends, family, are celebrating his life, trying not to cry
Looking back on treasured memories, that will never die
Aaron would have been proud, happy, of his final day
Knowing him, he would have had something to say

The day is over, we try to sleep, it's now the morning after
So peaceful, it's not the same, oh how we miss his laughter
Now this feeling of emptiness overcomes us, fills our heart
Thinking when is he coming back? We are not really apart

His room is still the same, his toys, books are all around
Bringing back the memories, oh look what we have found
These mementos and souvenirs cause so much distress
Tell us, how can we cope, control this feeling of emptiness

His pictures, holiday photographs, brings back memories
Our minds recall the good times, him telling us his stories
We see him in the garden, kicking a football, without a care
We come to our senses, suddenly realising he is not really there

We go to sleep, the feeling of emptiness temporarily disappears
In the morning, we awake, only to find this feeling reappears
To us it seems, this awful feeling will always be here to stay
We believe in time, it may fade, but it will never go away

At the end of September his sister will be going back to university
It will be just Mum and Dad at home, left to cope with any adversity
With just the two of us, the feeling of emptiness will become more real
We must continue to support each other, no matter how we may feel

JESUS

Found on Aaron's computer after his passing.

Inner Thoughts

In our quiet moments, our inner thoughts are running wild
Thinking, 'Why us? Why does it have to be our only boy child?'
I believe God must have had his reasons for taking him away
He must have done his deed on earth, he has had his day

At times, his absence overcomes us and the tears begin to flow
Oh Aaron, why you, why have you left us? Why did you have to go?
I miss you so much, it's so hard, you can't imagine what it's like
Thinking back to last summer, when we bought you a new bike

Mum's inner thoughts, it's summer holidays, we should be in the park
Riding your bike, with you falling off, having a laugh, having a lark
Why are you not here? Why is your bike in the garage gathering dust?
I can't understand, it's the Lord's judgement, to Him we have to trust

Without you it is so hard to get motivation, it is so hard to carry on
You were precious to us, our inspiration, now you are gone
How do we overcome this mental burden that could drag us down?
How do you remove the strains, the stresses, of not having you around?

Family and friends help us, by giving us their overwhelming support
We talk about you, read about you, from this we gain so much comfort
Yet still in our darkest moments, without you, there is so much loneliness
In our inner thoughts, we reflect on the past and recall such happiness

In the mornings I think, 'What am I working for? What is the purpose?'
The main reason was for my family, and you are not here with us
Deep down, I know, I must gain the mental toughness, I must persevere
For the sake of your mum and sister, after all, they are still here

I go to your grave, it's so peaceful, my problems seems to disappear
My inner thoughts tell me, it's because of you, Aaron, you are so near
I look down on you, think about you, remembering you in the past
It's you Aaron that is giving me the inner strength, it will always last

I also believe that no matter what happens in my future, with you gone
Nothing or no one can ever hurt me as much as the loss of my only son
Your death has changed us forever, it has given life a new perspective
I no longer worry about the future, that would have been your directive

I know death comes to all of us, but yours came sooner rather than later
I sometimes wish it would happen to me, so that we could be together
This is in my inner thoughts, although I still have some responsibilities
But nothing in life seems important any more, everything is trivialities

It's you that was motivating us, it's you that was our inspirational force
So although you are gone, you are still doing it, it is still you of course
You have left a huge void in our future life, it is now a test of endurance
My inner thoughts tell me you will always be there, to give us guidance

Memories of Life In Hospital

Looking back, there are so many memories that spring to mind
Of our life in the hospital with the people we have now left behind
Ward five was so congested, it had a unique family atmosphere
It was one for all, all for one, while we were virtually living there

We all had children with some form of cancer, we were in the same boat
Supporting each other, giving encouragement, just to keep us afloat
We all feel for our children, we were all staring potential death in the face
The camaraderie, the closeness was a vital element of life in the place

Sometimes we were on a high, having a laugh, something funny had occurred
Then you could sink into depths of despair as if your vision has been blurred
That is the roller coaster ride that was part of the life we were all enduring
The feeling of togetherness lifted you to ride the storm, to keep persevering

Aaron became the main man, the instigator of many hilarious situations
His cheeky comments and terrible jokes brought laughter on many occasions
He always wanted to know the life history of all the people he met
Then he would broadcast it to everyone else, he couldn't keep a secret

Caron's Crusade

On the oncology ward, Caron became Aaron's named nurse
It wasn't a match made in heaven, but it was for better or worse
Looking after Aaron wasn't easy, especially giving him his medicine
It became like a crusade, to win him over, to gain his confidence

Aaron was sometimes very impatient and tended to be very argumentative
Yet in your busy schedule, you kept your composure and were very attentive
In the end you convinced him you weren't the enemy, you were on his side
You won the crusade, supported him all the way to the end, you didn't hide

Julie Ruled

Julie, another nurse who looked after Aaron, she was very disciplined
She would march down the corridor to his bed, with his medicine
"Here you are," she would say, "I will be back in five minutes, I want it gone"
Aaron would try to argue, but she would stand no nonsense from our son

At last Aaron had met his match, she rules, they had a mutual understanding
Since we all know at times, our little man's attitude can be very demanding
It is strange, Julie left for a new position, as a nurse in the community
When he was home, guess who was his nurse? Mind you, there was an affinity

Raquel's Hell

There was a rather well-built Irish nurse, her name was Raquel
At times with his determined attitude, he could make her life hell
She was due to get married in August, at home in her native Ireland
Nosey Aaron as usual wanted to know, why she can't marry in England

Then out of the blue one day while Raquel was nursing him by his bed
Aaron made a very insulting and cheeky comment, this was what he said
"Are you going on a diet before the wedding?" I thought he was rather bold
"Why?" she asked. He replied, "So your husband can carry you over the
threshold!"

Obviously it was overheard, suddenly from silence came the laughing sound
Raquel replied, "Oh, you are so cheeky," she laughed herself, looking around
That episode was typical of Aaron, always causing us some embarrassment
Diplomacy was never his strong point, he would just make his own statement

Nina's Dilemma

There was also a young nurse named Nina, who he said walked like a penguin
They had an ongoing series of banter, so much to tell, where do I begin
He wanted to know all about her boyfriends, including the Peugeot man
Apparently, there was a different one for each day of the week, plus an extra one

If there is one thing with Aaron, he is not slow in coming forward
Pretty soon, "Nina's got eight boyfriends" was echoing around the ward
Nina was saying she hasn't got eight boyfriends, in her husky voice
Nevertheless, everyone in the ward will know, she hasn't got a choice

Luckily Nina has a sense of humour and accepted Aaron's taunting
If she didn't, her immediate personal future could be rather daunting
He kept going on and on, he better watch out or he could be in lumber
Then what happens, he goes and asks for her phone number

That one-liner brought a chorus of laughter, even to Nina's face
That was our Aaron, typical of him to bring some humour into the place
By the way, these eight boyfriends were a figment of Aaron's imagination
It was just another fictitious make believe, another of Aaron's invention

Marion's Chatter

Marion the Irish nurse on ward nine, like Aaron, she too was very talkative
One day Aaron was engrossed in a TV programme, he wasn't very receptive
Marion was chattering away in her Irish accent, the TV, he couldn't hear
Aaron was annoyed, the cause was Marion's chatter, this, he made quite clear

That was Aaron, straight to the point, you knew where you stood, no messing
Another typical situation, one of many, at times he can be so embarrassing
Marion knew where he was coming from, but she loved him, like all the rest
She brought him little presents, to keep his pecker up, after all, he was the best

Sarah's Saga

Sarah, another one of his favourite nurses, he asked her boyfriend's name
She was fond of him, like all the others, she teased him, playing a game
"His name is Aaron," he was laughing and then said, "I am not your boyfriend"
She replied "Well you are a special boy and you will always be my friend"

Sarah nicknamed him "Ugo" after a player from their favourite football team
They had many a discussion about their performances, they were the cream
One night she came into work, she was Aaron's nurse, she had to go home sick
Behind her back, Aaron was really telling her off, he gave her some real stick

If she wasn't very well, what did she come in for and tell me she is my nurse
He had a replacement nurse, someone he didn't know, that made it worse
She had to ask him for his hospital number, "I don't like her" was his reaction
So the next time Sarah came on duty, she had to give him a good explanation

Maggie's Eyebrows

There is another episode which occurred with Maggie, his hospital teacher
They developed a rapport, and teaching Aaron became a pleasure for her
He always asked awkward questions, always complaining if she was late
He looked forward to his lessons, so he moans, because he had to wait

Aaron sometimes is a master of the unexpected, even when his morale is low
Out of the blue he said to Maggie, "Don't you ever straighten your eyebrow"
She was rather taken aback, she rushed over to the mirror to have a look
Another off-the-cuff statement from Aaron, he was still engrossed in his book

Maggie appreciates that Aaron is so different, so observant, so outspoken
She takes the comment in her stride, no harm done, nothing has been broken
From then on she always checked her eyebrows, before starting the lesson
It is another memory to put in her bank, when she recalls her time with Aaron

Lorraine's Pain

There was a little girl named Alex, her brother Andrew and their mum Lorraine
Her mum thought Aaron was a right character, sometimes he was a right pain
She recalls Aaron singing, "Yummy, yummy, I have got a bug in my tummy"
He kept singing it all day after watching a video, he nearly drove her barmy

Her son Andrew was Aaron's playmate, he used to show him his card tricks
It kept Aaron occupied, trying them out, that is one way of getting some kicks
At night Aaron used to say "Lorraine, are you sleeping?" The reply? "I am not now."
She used to ask us, "Where have you got him from? He is something else, you know!"

A Welsh Nurse Error

There was an episode with a Welsh nurse, which caused an angry reaction
One day he started shivering and shaking, the cause was an infection
She said sorry, it was probably her fault, what a grave error to make
Aaron was absolutely furious, although those words were a mistake

So, he took his anger out on her because the shivers were frightening
He wasn't a happy man, his behaviour, wasn't one of understanding
Obviously, Aaron had gone over the top, she had been touching his line
Once the shivers had disappeared, he calmed down, he was now fine

I told Aaron she wasn't really responsible, he must apologise to her
Eventually, after some persuading, he said, "I am sorry," now that's better
She replied, "Oh, it is all right, my petal," in her pronounced Welsh accent
In the circumstances, Aaron just says things, he doesn't ask for your consent

The Pregnant Mum

Another scene which we didn't know about, till later on, well after the event
A new patient had arrived, her mum and dad were given the Aaron treatment
Apparently, Aaron was nosey as usual, asking her if she was fat or pregnant
So cheeky, they were probably wondering who is this guy, looking so innocent

One day in the new hospital, they brought the new baby along to show Aaron
That's what was in my tummy, I wasn't fat, this is our baby, a new-born son
That was when we first heard of Aaron's cheekiness, at least it was harmless
Later on, just before the end, the dad told me, your little son is something else

The Play Workers

The play workers are an integral part of the workforce and play an important role
Keeping the children happy and motivated, that is their main goal
These children with so many illnesses have temporarily lost their freedom
So playing games, doing puzzles, is so critical in relieving the boredom

Jade was the play worker on ward one, who helped to ease Aaron's frustration
She took time out to help and show him how to set up his beloved PlayStation
So on his first Christmas present, she became the first person to play a game
She can hold that memory, although now he has gone, things are not the same

Keran the play worker on the oncology ward, she gave him a syringe full of water
She was trying to relieve his fear of needles and if it hurts, he could squirt the doctor
This took all her powers of persuasion, to convince Aaron, it would be painless
She realises it was an ordeal for him, but eventually her comforting words were a success

Sandie the new play worker came onto the ward, she hadn't been there long
Aaron was always telling her off, whenever she had done something wrong
She remembers his honesty, his big broad smile on that very cheeky face
One that the passage of time, in her own memory, it will never erase

The Imaginary Husky Dogs

He also invented the husky dogs that were used to pull his wheelchair
They became an integral part of his life for a period, while he was in there
He gave two away, to Christine the physio and Charlotte from the BBC
They even had names and gave birth to little huskies you could never see

He was always asking, how were the huskies, concerned for their welfare
He was ensuring they were looked after, they were getting tender loving care
These things are fictitious examples that displayed our son's creativeness
Which helps him to overcome this ordeal and get through the healing process

The Eurovision Song Contest

The Eurovision song contest in Birmingham, this produced another funny occasion
Aaron and Raquel were teasing each other all day, they were in deep discussion
Raquel insisting Ireland has won it many times before and will win again tonight
There will be many Irish people in Birmingham to see this wonderful sight

Aaron insisted he must go to the National Indoor Arena in his wheelchair
He wanted to see all the foreigners and some Irish people, if they were there
So that afternoon off we went to the arena with him talking to people we met
Wanting to know where they came from, once known, he wouldn't forget

He shouted to one gentleman, "Are you Dutch?" "No," came the reply, "I am German"
Further along the road, he was talking aloud, "I can't find anyone from Ireland"
Suddenly an Irish voice echoed, "I am Irish," it came completely out of the blue
Aaron was surprised, at last an Irishman, talking Irish, asking, "Who are you?"

They had a chat, introduced themselves, he gave him a programme of the show
Aaron was pleased as punch, he had met an Irishman, his face all aglow

He could now go back to the hospital and tell everyone of his little adventure
Listening to him going on and on, to their ears it must have been sheer torture

That evening he watched the show, following the songs, the programme in hand
It was in different languages, reading the words, it was difficult to understand
He is fascinated by countries of the world, so he gave the show all his attention
Although he was very disappointed at the result, the United Kingdom hadn't won

Other Memories

Once Aaron was in his wheelchair, he would go wandering off, leaving his mum
Telling her he will be back soon, he has gone to play with his hospital chums
His mum didn't mind, she could have some peace and quiet, even read a book
On these occasions, Aaron was up to his escapades, she didn't think to look

Aaron was beginning to think he was a star, he wanted to do his own documentary
So with a recorder and a microphone, he would go around
doing a running commentary
People hearing this voice coming from behind, surprised,
they turned around, it was Aaron
He would ask them questions, conducting an interview with the staff as he went along

He would ask them questions about the hospital and the patients
Recording their answers, then play it back, laughing at their comments
The reply from Mrs Kenyon the care worker was especially funny
This was just another example of Aaron's inventiveness, one of many

There was another occasion, we weren't aware of, until very later on
One evening, Aaron was in the parents' room on his own with the television on
He was watching "Moll Flanders", something his mum would never allow
In walked a parent and caught him red-handed, engrossed in this show

He was surprised, asking her not to tell his mum, she didn't know he was there
"She thinks I am with my mates on the PlayStation," there was a little sign of fear
When this mum told us the story, we all had to laugh, it was so typical of Aaron
But that is her memory of him to keep, to remember now that he has moved on

Aaron the joker, also liked to play practical jokes on people he knew
So, one night he put a rubber snake in James grandmother's bed, she hadn't a clue
Unsuspecting, pulling back the blankets, to be greeted by a snake, not a pretty sight
Aaron was laughing his head off, she jumped out of her skin, giving her quite a fright

Ron, little Nellie's dad, was always telling weird and wonderful stories
Gathering around waiting for the punchline are special memories
He would have Aaron jumping or in stitches, he couldn't stop laughing
With Aaron's infectious laughter, his whole body seems to be vibrating

There was also a big Black Country gentleman, whose name I can't remember
His daughter was in and out for treatment, she was a temporary ward member
Aaron's talking and knowledge gave the impression, he was Mister Know-it-all
Once he said to him, "I can't stand smart little kids, who think they know it all"

This was all part of the humour, that helps to release the pressure we all feel
We are all concerned for our children's welfare in a situation far from ideal
Another scene where his friends helped was getting hot cross buns for Aaron
Not really difficult if it was Easter, but trying to get them in December is not on

Marion, one of his favourite nurses, tried to find some, without any success
A really nice Black Country lady on the ward, said she would try her best
She had a broad Black Country accent, so funny, it was yam this and yam that
We were lucky, she found some buns, Aaron is happy, thank goodness for that

There was an occasion when he was in the high-dependency unit, in isolation
He put a list of names of who could enter his room without asking for his permission
Dr Hansel came in, asking why Dr Stevenson name was on and he is not there
He just said, "Dr Stevenson is the boss, he doesn't need permission to come in here"

Dr Hansel wasn't surprised by Aarons comment, it brought a smile to his face
He knows Aaron is displaying his upfront style, after so many months in this place
Similarly, when an unknown lady was looking at his file, without introducing herself
He just came out with, "Excuse me, who are you?" she apologised to the man himself

Aaron always wanted to know who his nurse was at every shift changeover
If he didn't know her, he would complain and go to see Trish the ward sister
He would tell her, "You're the boss, it is your decision, why can't I have you?"
She would reply, "We have to share you around, they are all fighting over you"

Basically, they all wanted to nurse Aaron, they know he was so funny
He would make them laugh, tell them off, but he was good company
That is Aaron's attraction, he could never be accused of being boring
His inquisitive nature, other people's minds he was always exploring

Yet my overall memory of Aaron was him being the leader on the ward
Because of his upfront style, he came across a bit like a shop steward
If the children had any problems with the staff, he would sort them out
If he wasn't satisfied, I had a vision of him leading them on a walkout

Mum and Dad

---★---

The impact of Aaron's illness on Mum and Dad was one of devastation
To see your son as a healthy child to one so ill gives a feeling of deflation
It is so difficult to come to terms with such a drastic change in your life
Living through a nightmare was a mental anguish for me, and my wife

Yet from the moment he became ill, it was only his welfare we had at heart
It didn't matter to us, although we knew as man and wife, we would be apart
Mum had to be with him, that's definite, he is her baby, he is our little man
He is the number one priority, whatever it takes, we will do all we can

So the scenario is set, Mum will have to give up work, to be with her son
She will always be there to care and cuddle him, be there to be called on
Dad will have to keep working, life has to go on, bills still have to be paid
It wasn't planned, it wasn't self-inflicted, it just happened, it wasn't made

So dad's daily cycle was work, hospital, canteen food, home to sleep, it is a test
Often falling asleep in the armchair, too tired for bed, to have a proper rest
Besides, after sleeping with the one you love for twenty-four years or more
It is difficult to sleep on your own, not for this long, it's never happened before

Even though you are mentally and physically tired, at times it is hard to sleep
Your body needs to, but your brain is in turmoil, it doesn't work counting sheep
This routine changed at weekends, when Mum came home to do some chores
Dad looked after his son, often falling asleep with him, the son he adores

It was also very hard for Mum, she has to see him in whatever condition he is in
She deserves all the plaudits, she has the patience of a saint, that never wore thin
She has to put up with Aaron's moods, caused by the medication in his current
state
Yet through it all she never wilted, a tower of strength in a horrendous climate

During this time, it got worse, her car was stolen from outside the hospital
Her means of getting home, has been taken away, something that was so vital
Obviously there are people, who couldn't care less about others' predicament
Yet to us it's trivial in the circumstances, Aaron's life was far more important

All this put more strain on Dad, who had to take Mum to and from the hospital
But our friends helped us out, their contribution to the cause was so essential
It does test your resolve to the limit, but you find the strength to carry on
Anyway, you haven't got a choice, you just keep going for the sake of our son

It is not just the logistics of not having Mum's car that puts pressure on you
To rectify the problem, it is the paperwork and phone calls you have to do
Whoever was responsible, obviously those people haven't got a conscience
Not knowing, that what they have done, has caused us so much inconvenience

Sometimes we had arguments, caused by the pressure, the stress of it all
It is just the tiredness surfacing, you need a release, otherwise you could fall
Yet above all this, the love we share, the love for our son, keeps you going
Although at times, you are totally exhausted, you are running on adrenaline

For months my wife and I were what you call passing strangers in the night
Only the occasional Saturday afternoon together at home, gave us some respite
Those precious moments, courtesy of Kath and Dot, gave us the time to reflect
On the situation, the pressure we are under, how to overcome it, what to expect

All through his illness, we thought he would pull through, we were optimistic
Obviously, he may have some physical disability, you also have to be realistic
The disability we can handle, although we are hoping it doesn't affect his brain
That is his strength, but if it did, we would still cope under a tremendous strain

All these thoughts go through your mind during this heartbreaking period
You keep thinking, he is going to be all right, but these thoughts you can't avoid
Sadly, in the end it didn't matter, his sudden demise, came as a terrible shock
You see him motionless, so peaceful, wishing you could turn back the clock

At the end of the day our strong relationship carried us through to the sad ending
In the future, this strength must continue, for on each other we are depending
Aaron may not be here in body and soul, but he is still here with us in our mind
We look for reasons, explanations for his death, but the reasons you can't find

The familiar phrase "Only the good die young" and in his case, that is so true
It is proven on the screen, the pictures never lie, it has been shown to all of you
To us it is no consolation, deep down inside, we will always feel some pain
But his tributes are so comforting, he has left a legacy, he didn't die in vain

These tributes, family and friends, helps us to cope with the grieving process
Trying hard to keep our sanity, trying hard not to get too depressed
But at times it is so difficult, you feel you want to give up, throw in the towel
We think of our little man, deep down that is one thing he wouldn't allow

So in his physical absence, we still have to continue our life, living from day to day
But mentally he will always be here, the precious memories will never go away
We have to hold on to those, they are what keep us going, keep us alive
Without them and our daughter, we would find it so difficult to cope, to survive

Finally, to our respective employers they were so flexible, also so helpful
To allow time off during the last year for our son, we are extremely grateful
We thank you and all those people who supported us through to the conclusion
Although it wasn't what we desired, there wasn't a choice, it wasn't our decision

**A FAMILY PHOTOGRAPH, SHOWING AARON
THE NEW CUB SCOUT
WITH HIS MUM, DAD AND SISTER**

HE CALLED US THE GLASSES FAMILY

Sister Theresa

⭐

Aaron's illness was difficult for his sister, Theresa, he was her only brother
As children growing up, they loved, they fought and argued with each other
The seriousness, the life or death situation was hard for her to comprehend
Although they were family, brother and sister, he was also her friend

During Aaron's long illness she was at university, away from the daily events
Not seeing what is happening, what he is going through,
not seeing his predicaments
It must have been so difficult for her to concentrate, away in a new environment
Knowing her brother is in hospital, undergoing all kinds of tests and treatment

She came home, regularly at weekends and holidays to be there for him
It was so mentally draining for her to see him, at times it was looking grim
He always looked forward to seeing her, deep down he was so proud of her
At least for a short while, although they still argued, they could be together

Deep down, we believe Theresa wanted to be here, during his long illness
We told her, it is better for her to be away, for her not to see him in distress
Aaron wanted her to continue her education and obtain her degree
It is a difficult situation, you are between the Devil and the deep blue sea

We know Aaron wouldn't want to be the one responsible for her not continuing
She couldn't really do much up here, in fact for her, it could be soul-destroying
We told her to confide in someone, someone who could give her help and support
At times she will need it, a shoulder to lean on, to give her words of comfort

After her first year she came back for the summer, when Aaron was at home
A family united again, after nine months apart, welcome Theresa, welcome
She got herself a summer job, things were looking up, at least for a while
Sadly, it didn't last long, it was shattered by Aaron's death on that day in July

That devastated all of his family, we cried together, we all shed many a tear
Theresa was feeling guilty, for being away from him, during his last year
As we explained to her, nothing would have been achieved by her presence
Nevertheless, she found it difficult to come to terms with her absence

Back in the early days, we didn't know what the final outcome would be
We couldn't forecast what was going to happen to Aaron, we couldn't foresee
So in the end, the right thing was to continue her studies and do her best
Strange that her results came, dated the same day he died, she passed the test

To The Hospital Staff, Thank You

★

To all the hospital staff, who helped and nursed Aaron you were all dedicated
From our family your patience, to try to get him better, is greatly appreciated
All we can say, you all did everything you could possibly do to keep him alive
In the end, it wasn't enough, we still thank you, although he failed to survive

You all accepted his temperamental changes and refusing do as he was told
You all showed a great deal of perseverance, you all have memories to hold
These memories maybe happy or sad, they may make you laugh, or even cry
But there is one thing for sure, they will be remembered, they will never die

Some of you were filmed in the presence of the little man himself, the shining star
On the screen, you can see yourselves, nursing and helping him to come so far
Therefore you will have visual memories to hang on to, to see as time goes by
They may inspire you in the future, as you recall the scenes, the pictures never lie

To Caron his named nurse on the cancer ward, you deserve a special mention
You were the main one, who really had to coerce him to take his medication
This made you very unpopular with him, but you took it all in your stride
He tested your patience, you never wilted, you didn't try to hide

Therefore, from us, a special thank you for nursing him, through to the end
Aaron apologised to you before the end came, we know you were his friend
To Dr Stevenson his main cancer consultant, you also deserve a special mention
You did all you could, you were the main one he was always asking a question

As far as we are concerned, Dr Stevenson is the best, a credit to his profession
His dedication to the cause, in trying to save lives, leaves a lasting impression
You were considerate, you took time out to explain everything to us, in detail

We know you were very sorry, it wasn't a success, but to us you haven't failed

To you, our sincere thanks, at the end of day you couldn't have done any more
We know you miss our little man, answering one last question, then no more
But we know in this type of environment for every failure there is one success
Aaron hasn't died in vain, his case study will help others, with a similar illness

To Deena and Mo the dietician, full marks for patience in trying to get him to eat
To Christine the physiotherapist, who really tried to get him back on his feet
To his teachers, doctors, nurses, play workers, carers, domestics, a final thank you
Our family are eternally grateful and have nothing but respect for all of you

To The Visitors And Family, Thank You

───────── ★ ─────────

To the visitors who came to see Aaron during this heartbreaking ordeal
You all visited him in all kinds of weather, in a situation far from ideal
Your presence, your overwhelming support, helped us to see it through
It was all greatly appreciated and we send you all a sincere thank you

There are a lot of people who deserve special thanks, where do I start?
I will begin with his schoolmates, they visited often and played their part
From the onset their parents offered their help, anything they could do
They knew his friends were vital, for his morale, to help him pull through

The regular visitors were: Julie came with Jonathon, Liz came with James
They brought him presents, kept him in touch with school, played his games
Leslie came with Alice, with their presents, along with Karen and Elliot,
Janet also came with little Stacey, more presents, oh what a lot he has got

There was Clary with Jamie, plus Nicholas and his mum Kay
They came, with more presents, to cheer him up, to give him a happy day
Sandra came with Jonathon, he knew Aaron from when they were toddlers
They had always kept in touch, went to each other's parties as they got older

These visits from his chums, were to make Aaron feel he hasn't being forgotten
They gave him something to look forward to, even when he was feeling rotten
They kept him in touch with what was happening outside, the latest news
He could talk to them, tell them about his own situation, express his views

His teachers from the infant school also came to see their former pupil
Their presence and words of encouragement all helps the little one who is so ill

Mrs Holgan his teacher came and also with Mrs Payton his last headmistress
They all brought gifts to cheer him up, trying to help him to overcome his illness

Mum's friends from the Methodist church came regularly to give her support
Along with Rev. Sampson her minister, these visits gave us great comfort
They were praying for our little man to get better, along with so many others
We say thank you to them, after all, in this world, we are all sisters and brothers

His Sunday school teacher came plus his Beaver pals with their leader Lyn
He needed to be kept in touch with what is going on, what is happening
But there are two special people to mention, that is Kath his godmother
Dot his mum's long-standing friend from the Methodist church is the other

AARON'S THANK YOU LETTER TO AUNTIE KATH
HIS GODMOTHER

31 Robert Av

Erdington

Birmingha

B23 5RD

March 10th

Dear Kath

I love you still but, I just wanted to say thank-you for giving me the sads book. I also like to know when are your coming to Visit and play games. Next time can I do the sad please.

Love
Aaron xxxx
K S H M

They both came in emergencies, when his mum was under unbearable strain
They were a shoulder to cry on, an umbrella to protect her from the pouring rain
There was also Mavis, Dad's work colleague, she came on a regular basis
To give her support, she was fond of Aaron, always willing to help and assist

There was his little friend Cleo and her dad Wade, he was Aaron's godfather
She came with us on our last holiday, the last time they played together
They had known each other since they were toddling around the house
Many times they would fall out, like children do, then make up and still be close

JC and Marilyn, Dad and Mum's long-standing friends, going back thirty years
They even came to give their support, with Dad trying to hold back the tears
This just shows how real friendship can mean so much, in times of sadness
A true friend is there for you, in times of need, helping to overcome this madness

As well as all these friends, who were there for us, for Aaron our little man
We mustn't forget his family, his relatives, they supported us as only they can
There was Auntie Novy, an ex-nurse, she was also there, to give his mum relief
It gave her a chance to return to nursing, temporarily, although it was only brief

Grandma, Nanny and Granddad, they came to visit the grandson they had
To see Aaron in this condition, in distress, at times it seems so sad
Auntie Pat and her husband Scott, with cousins Dionne and Dominque
They came regularly with Suzanne, Dad's niece and her daughter Natalie

Uncle Tony, his wife Mandy, baby Bradley, a new cousin along with Kellyann
They all came, along with Uncle Bobby, all are family you are able to rely on
There was his Uncle Chris, his wife Anna and cousin Laura their daughter
Uncle Kingsley, his wife Lauverne, cousins Benjamin, Stephanie and Jennifer

There were also many handmade cards, from his classmates at school
Telling him to get well soon, saying how much they missed him, Mr Cool
These gestures were so precious to Aaron, for him to maintain his motivation
They gave him hope, they gave him an incentive to overcome his situation

Knowing all these people were there for him, they gave him a tremendous lift
For Aaron it was so vital, your presence was more important than the gifts
Finally, maybe there are some people that I have forgotten, in addition to those above
Aaron's Mum, Dad and Sister, thank you all for visiting and showing your love

To The BBC, Thank You

───── ★ ─────

When the BBC started filming in the hospital with Aaron having a central part
He loved it, it kept him going, he enjoyed every moment, from the very start
It did him good, it distracted him from the treatment, helped him see it through
To them, the producers, directors and cameramen, we have to say thank you

They spent many hours filming, I suppose, they thought, they were a nuisance
To us and especially for Aaron's well-being, we were happy with their presence
Charlotte the director, probably thought when she first met our eight-year-old
What an overwhelming personality, so inquisitive, so courageous, so very bold

They soon built up a mutual friendship, they were probably good for each other
The filming kept Aaron occupied, at every opportunity they would be together
With Aaron's strong character, you could begin to think who is directing who
She let him get on with it, he is the boss, follow him, see what he is going to do

Aaron let the filming go to his head, he soon thought he was a television star
He had his own hospital fan club, the cameras were never far away, never far
Many people wanted to be filmed with Aaron, wanting to be part of the scene
They could see themselves on television, with a star, our Aaron, on the screen

There are so many terrific scenes, the editing must have been really difficult
He could have had his own series, never mind, we are happy with the end result
He was thinking, he will be back at school when the programme goes out
His mates will be asking for an autograph of a star they could shout about

From what we have seen, the scenes have captured our Aaron in his element
His personality comes shining through, he would have had the star treatment
He was an inspiration, for the other children, he showed he was concerned
He wasn't always thinking of himself, there is so much we have all learnt

The sad part is, he won't be here to see the end result, his debut on the TV
He would have been a star, now it is only the ones left behind who will see

Our little man in the limelight, saying his one-liners and it is all for free
He would have been proud, laughing at the scenes, sadly it wasn't meant to be

So thank you to the BBC for choosing Aaron, especially to Jane and Charlotte
You have given our family visual memories, ones that we will never ever forget
I am sure others will gain strength from seeing Aaron's inspirational qualities
Strength to face life's adversities, strength to overcome life's harsh realities

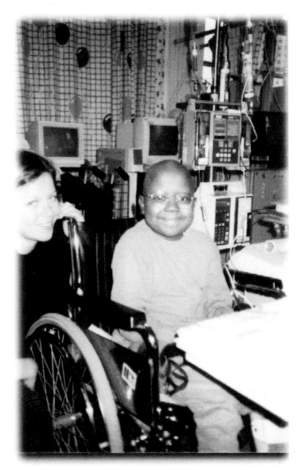

AARON AND CHARLOTTE, THE BBC PRODUCER

THEY BECAME FIRM FRIENDS,
DURING THE PRODUCTION OF THE SERIES,
SHE CAPTURED HIS TRUE PERSONALITY ON THE SCREEN

Aaron and Nellie

Nellie came into the ward, it wasn't long before Aaron made himself known
He wanted to know all about her, that's our son, he wouldn't leave her alone
Ron and Lou her parents were subjected to Aaron's questioning technique
They soon realise what have we got here, he is a bit different, he is unique

It didn't take long for a friendship to develop, although she is only two
Aaron became her best friend, a shoulder to lean on, someone he could read to
Their beds were side by side, I suppose you could say, they were neighbours
A bond developed between them, Aaron was encouraging, doing her favours

They watched videos together, especially Nellie's favourite "Pete's Dragon"
She had to watch this every morning regardless, a necessity, it had to be on
She also had to watch the "Fun Factory", she had to have her daily dose
After a while Aaron would say, "Oh no not again!" It's natural, I suppose

Being a little lady, she had to have priority over the video and television
Being a gentleman, Aaron didn't really argue, that was his decision
Whenever he wasn't around, Nellie would miss him, where has he gone?
In her baby voice, her catchphrase, she was always saying "Where is Aaron?"

Looking back now you can recall so many happy times and funny situations
A scene from the "The Lion, the Witch and the Wardrobe" was one occasion
Suddenly Aaron from looking intense, he burst into tears, he really cried
He took it serious, he thought one of the central characters had really died

Ron and Lou tried to console him, explain that he will be coming back alive
Aaron didn't believe them, until at the end, he came back, he had survived
His face changed from sadness to howls of laughter, gone were his tears
Ron thought it was so funny, he will never forget, if he lives a hundred years

As time went by our family became firm friends, Aaron was Ron's mate
It is amazing how an eight-year-old and a grown man can really relate
That is the strange thing about Aaron, the age gap was not a barrier
He could hold a conversation with old and young alike, age didn't matter

Aaron and Nellie became television stars, they were often filmed together
With Aaron reading Nellie a story, "Little Miss Sunshine", both in laughter
That scene was used to launch the television series, it is a beautiful picture
One to keep, one to treasure, one to bring back happy memories, in the future

It is amazing how that beautiful picture sends out a message, nothing phony
Innocent eight and two-year-old, black and white united, in perfect harmony
Telling the world in sickness and in health, we can smile, we can live as one
It portrays Aaron's life, that would be his wish for the future, now he's gone

Another scene with Aaron which demonstrates his true concern for Nellie
Was when she returned, with a high temperature, this scene was shown on telly
On this occasion, there was a shortage of beds, so they couldn't be together
When Aaron heard that his little friend was back in, he couldn't wait to see her

So off he goes, bursting through the door with his rollator, with cameras behind
He was in a hurry, she was in another ward, his little friend, he had to find
When he found her, he couldn't talk, he was panting like mad, gasping for air
Ron said with a smile, "Calm down mate," Nellie was on the bed, sitting over there

He went across to sit by Nellie, she was playing with something called music
"What's music?" asked Aaron, it appears that music to Nellie is really lipstick
This brought out a typical Aaron laugh as he proceeded to put some on her lips
Nellie smiled and said her phrase "I like Aaron", she was attached to her drips

We believe these scenes with Nellie are ones to remember, are ones to treasure
During that period in hospital, we were a family, they gave so much pleasure
The friendship was mutually rewarding for both families, it kept us motivated
We were all thinking positively, although at times our emotions often fluctuated

Looking back, we were all hoping this true friendship would be there forever
Nellie and Aaron growing up, keeping in touch, recalling their times together
They have both been through so much, took it all with a smile on their faces
Sadly, Aaron isn't here, I am sure he is looking over Nellie from a better place

Although Aaron has gone to heaven, we keep in touch with Nellie, Ron and Lou
Nellie is still fighting this disease, we hope she successfully sees it through
It is so strange, that now he has gone, Nellie no longer says, "Where is Aaron!"
It is as if deep down in her little mind, she knows her friend has moved on

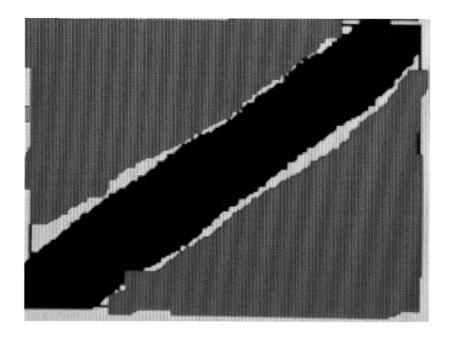

FLAG OF TRINIDAD AND TOBAGO

Aaron was fascinated with the world this flag was found on the computer after his passing.

Aaron and Baby James

Baby James had contracted leukaemia, so young, he was only a few months old
Aaron soon adopted him as his hospital brother, one to cuddle, one to hold
They were neighbours for such a long while, they took their treatment together
Aaron loved him, he was always concerned for him, his new-found brother

As he couldn't look after himself, as he was totally dependent for loving care
If Aaron was mobile and feeling well, he would go to play with him, in his wheelchair
When he returned to the new hospital, he gave him a cuddle and a kiss
His affection for him was there to be seen, the little one, he had missed

Aaron and Victoria

———— ★ ————

There was Victoria and her mum Carol, he caught shingles, so he blamed her
So, he ended up in the high-dependency unit, segregated, but closer to her
Aaron worked out that the phones were linked, it was a means of communication
Therefore, he was always on the phone, chatting away, in a serious conversation

He explained what to do if you are having a MRI scan and wanted a wee
All you have to do is shake a leg is what I done, so that they could see
What a topic of conversation to discuss with Victoria, can you believe it?
With Aaron anything goes, he is innocent, at least he's still maintaining his wit

Carol exchanged some sweets with Aaron, which she keeps as a lasting reminder
Of her little friend, who created quite an impression on her, husband and daughter
Her lasting memory of Aaron was she was the last person to share his secret
She says, you think of him and you have to smile, so Aaron she will never forget

Aaron and Jadon

—— ★ ——

When Aaron vacated his room, it was taken over by a six-year-old from Stoke
He had Non-Hodgkin lymphoma like Aaron, this is a serious illness, is not a joke
His name was Jadon, with his mum Maria, dad Nick, brothers Wayne and Stuart
They soon became part of our hospital family, in despair, we were a happy lot

Aaron soon became Jadon's friend, his mate, a true friend who really cared
Jadon was bedridden in the early days, Aaron was concerned for his welfare
He was always asking how he was, visited him in his room, once he was mobile
A true friendship grew, they were in the same boat, they were here for a while

His brothers were also his friends, they played with him throughout his illness
It was just what he wanted, to distract him, to stop him from getting depressed
They used to play football games on his PlayStation, staying up late at night
Sometimes arguing, just typical children, falling out, debating what is right

Eventually, in a special wheelchair, Jadon was allowed to leave his room
He would go past Aaron's bed in the morning on his way to the playroom
His phrase "Gordon Bennett, he is still kipping?" is something to remember
A character in his own right, a brave lad, to the family a valuable member

His brothers became his fan club, while Aaron was being filmed for the TV
They tried to get in on the act, there in the background for everyone to see
Jadon also played with Aaron's PlayStation, occasionally you heard a shout
In his excitement, his catchphrase "Gordon Bennett" would come ringing out

When Aaron was being discharged, he will be temporarily parted from his friend
We were happy and sad, little did we know, they will be together in the end
On the day we left, Aaron said goodbye, he remarked, "Jadon is the king now"
Aaron has relinquished his throne, passed it to Jadon, he has taken his final bow

When Aaron relapsed and finally passed away, Jadon's family shared our grief
They were in the same situation, it could happen to them, with no signs of relief
They cried with us, Jadon wanted to see us, he has just lost one of his best mates
A week later they will be together again, in that playground in the sky, it is fate

Sadly, Jadon followed Aaron and passed away the day after Aaron's funeral
They are now in heaven together, arguing who is going to be king, the General
We can imagine the two of them surrounded by little children, all playing together
With Aaron and Jadon leading the way, running around in all kinds of weather

Looking back at our lives on the ward, fighting the disease, at times in despair
In our minds, in our moments of depression, we are thinking, life just isn't fair
Yet we feel for his family, he was looking well, we really hoped he would survive
Now we are grieving together as one, with only happy memories to keep them alive

Aaron and Del

One day the TV news said Del, a girl from Ireland, was coming to the hospital
She was coming over for life changing operations, to save her life, it was vital
Aaron immediately took an interest, already he was showing concern for Del
Pretty soon he wanted to meet her, this little girl, who hasn't been very well

Charlotte from the BBC took him in his wheelchair, one afternoon, to see her
So after waiting for her to feel better, at last they could meet and be together
A mutual friendship developed in no time at all, they got on like a house on fire
It is funny how they were once two strangers, now each other they can inspire

That inspiration hopefully will see them through, see them both get well
They have a long way to go, as parents, that is all we want for Aaron and Del
Although they have different illnesses, they both show a tremendous will to win
The courage to fight their predicament, the strength coming out from within

The friendship developed, although they were apart and couldn't be together
They kept in touch and started communicating, by writing letters to each other
With Sandie the play worker acting as the post lady, she was the go-between
It seems like a hospital romance was in the air, you can imagine the scene

Sadly her last letter with a gift for Aaron, to which he was too poorly to reply
He was coming to the end of his short life, a situation so sad, you could cry
She had already given him a card of her favourite football team's autographs
Mum and Dad went to see her, gave her a gift from Aaron and his photograph

Del was looking really well, after undergoing such a pioneering operation
Her inner strength brought her this far, after years of coping with her situation
It seems her and our Aaron had strong personalities, they were two of a kind
Both outspoken, both expressing their feelings, to whom, they didn't mind

Her mum recalled when she first met Aaron, he was firing questions at her

He was going so fast, he hardly gave her time to think, to give him an answer
That is another example of our little man, seemingly having a one-way discussion
Nevertheless, if there is one thing guaranteed, he always leaves an impression

She has been to the edge and back, she has been on a journey of discovery
We sincerely hope Del continues improving, continues her road to recovery
Part of that journey was meeting our son Aaron, now physically they are apart
She told us she keeps his picture in her pocket, because it is close to her heart

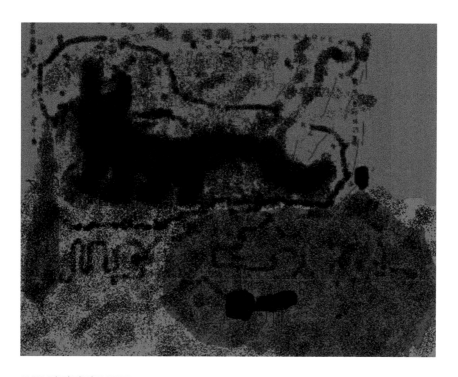

UNTITLED

Found on Aaron's computer after his passing.

Aaron and His Other Hospital Friends

There were many other children and parents, who were attracted to Aaron
Due to the length of time he was in hospital, the list could go on and on
But there are few that were in and out of hospital regularly that come to mind
They grew fond of him, they loved his upfront style, they were also very kind

There was Jennica, a little toddler, and her dad Cal. Aaron called him his mate
Aaron's cheeky comments would have Cal in laughter, he was in a right state
Sometimes from behind the curtain, the quietness would be shattered by a roar
Another of Aaron's gems would have him laughing, almost till he hit the floor

Another lady, she was attracted to Aaron, a domestic, her name was Rina
She came to see him at every opportunity, he was always glad to see her
She gave him every encouragement to help him overcome his illness
She was there during good times, she was there when he was in distress

Loria, another domestic, became someone to talk to, a close friend
Supporting us all the way through this sad journey to the very end
She came to his funeral to pay her last respects, to say goodbye
Along with all the other mourners, she was trying hard not to cry

Paul, the nurse on ward one, he and Aaron would have many a debate
He would tell him some unbelievable stories, Aaron was his mate
The age difference wasn't a barrier, as they engaged in serious conversation
The discussions were intense, with Aaron giving him an inquisition

To the other friends whom Aaron was attracted to during his stay in hospital
All I can say, your contribution to his life there, for his moral, it was so vital

I know Aaron gave the parents his questioning technique, the third degree
But that is our little man, the life and soul of the party, so inquisitive, you see

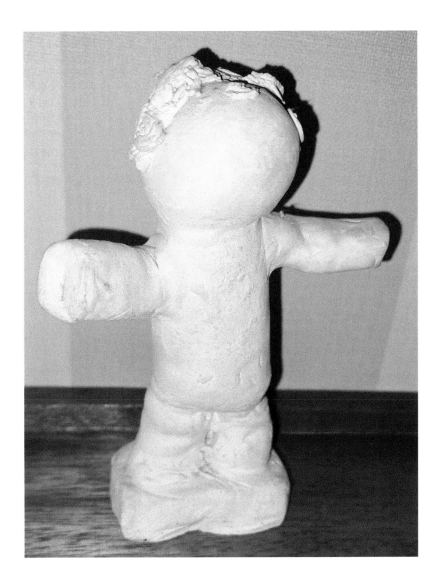

Aaron's School Handiwork

Aaron

Aaron was our little boy, who became our little man by the age of eight
He was destined to be someone special, someone who would be really great
This was confirmed by the reaction from the TV series, it was there to be seen
He could have been anything he wanted to be, that came across on the screen

He was a boy with many attributes, a unique style, a larger-than-life character
A loveable rogue, whether he was serious or funny, you would be in fits of laughter
An inspiration, with an aura about him, sometimes he would even sing you a song
So special, with his attitude, his determination, he wouldn't be down for long

His bravery in the face of adversity was one of his major characteristics
A true soldier, in the true sense of the word, he could be termed charismatic
His strength to bounce back and maintain his cheerful, humorous nature
After taking such punishing treatment was amazing, to see him was a picture

He loved geography, the world, the countries and its people was his passion
He studied the capitals, the animals and wildlife, he was a mine of information
His greatest wish was to go to France and to Paris, that was his fascination
He always had his pencil and notepad, he was a writer with a vivid imagination

His smile and laughter will be remembered in the viewers' memory banks
It is to him that we are all thankful, it is to him we have to give our thanks
An exceptional child who achieved so much in his eight years on God's land
More than some people will achieve in eighty, I am sure you will understand

LITTLE MAN
**A TRIBUTE TO AARON (OUR LITTLE MAN),
SHOWING HIS CLASSIC POSE,
CAPTURED AND DRAWN BY THE FATHER
OF ONE OF HIS SCHOOLMATES.**

Aaron, The Tv Star

Now that he has gone, he has left behind a legacy
Aaron is now a TV star, sadly himself, he can't see
In September, he will be screened on the telly
He will be shown nationwide, with his mate Nellie

As parents we were in two minds whether to put it out
There was really no choice, that there is no doubt
He would have wanted to, that is him, that's his style
He came across so natural, with his infectious smile

The hours he spent filming have been edited down
They have still captured him, even his frown
His charismatic personality was an inspiration
Now he is spreading it all across the nation

He will give many people some kind of hope
Showing with his illness, you can still cope
His memory on the screen, he has left behind
That is typical of him, so thoughtful, so kind

To the people who are with him on the screen
Memories are there, memories that can be seen
They will probably have a smile and have a cry
He has left mixed emotions, that will never die

Aaron certainly wasn't born to be anonymous
The reaction from the show has made him famous
A shining example, to all, who watched the show
The curtain is closed, he has taken his final bow

We will have to find the strength to watch the show
It will bring back so many memories, you know

With the passage of time, we will find the courage
To watch him, to see again, to see his visual image

He is up in heaven, looking down, still a star
A legend in his own lifetime, a legend by far
It is so sad, he can't see himself, in all his glory
It wasn't meant to be, that's life, it is Aaron's story

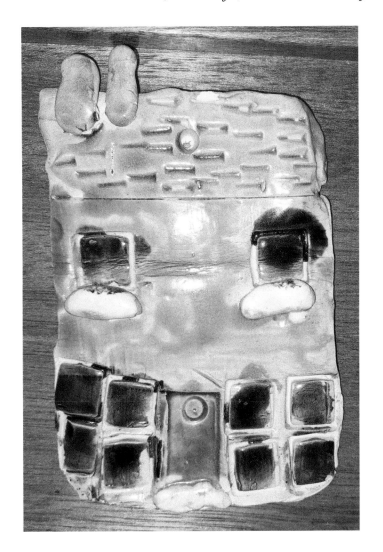

Aaron's School Handiwork

The Future

———— ★ ————

From birth, Aaron was our life, he was the boss of the household
It is hard to believe he has gone, such a loss, we have to be bold
We have to pick up our life without him and return to normality
Try to come to terms with his absence, it is not a dream, it is reality

In our minds, we think of all the things we would be doing
To see Aston Villa play, that's where we would be going
Also to play golf, pulling Dad's trolley, just being his caddy
Instead of going shopping with Mum, no I am going with Daddy

We wonder what he would have become, in the years ahead
He wanted to go to the University of Aston, is what he always said
With his determination, his achievements would have been great
It wasn't meant to be, life can be so cruel, it must be his fate

Saturday afternoons, we miss him, it will never be the same
Watching the TV, for the football results, following every game
He would be shouting "Yes, yes" if his favourite team has won
It's these little things that are hard to bear, now that he has gone

Everything we do in the future, without him, will seem so unreal
Going to Sunday school with his mum, she misses him, it's an ordeal
Visiting Grandma with his dad, seeing his cousins, to keep in touch
To do these things for the first time, suddenly becomes all too much

All the things father and son do together, during the growing process
Are gone forever, it really hurts inside, you can become so depressed
When you lose your son, you lose your friend, your future companion
From the father's viewpoint, in his mind, everything is an imagination

He would be saying, "Mum, is dinner ready?" That's his normal behaviour
With him not being here with us, even the food lacks a touch of flavour

Now there is one less mouth to feed, one less around the dinner table
He would be making comments about his food, it is so uncomfortable

In a short time, our happy family of four has been reduced by a quarter
Coming to terms with his absence is so hard, but we have our daughter
His sister is our living future now, we have to carry on for her sake
Although it is so easy to give up, we know this would be a mistake

We go away for a few days, we got lost trying to find the caravan park
You would be moaning, saying are we going to find it before it is too dark
In the park there are other children running around, playing in the pool
You would have been there with them, meeting new friends, looking so cool

Everything we do for the first time, without you, it is so hard to bear
Even going to the dentist, with visions of you, mouth open in the chair
You would be looking into our mouth, so close we are almost kissing
These are the little things, the future brings, the things we are missing

Your birthday comes around, we receive cards and take flowers to your grave
We think of you, the precious one, the love you had and the love you gave
You were one in a million to us, but our hearts are filled with so much sorrow
We are still grieving for you, we take one day at a time, not thinking of tomorrow

Christmas will be difficult without you, so for us it will be tough to survive
We will be thinking back to the previous Christmas in hospital, your last one alive
So with you not being here with us, how can we celebrate, the answer is we cannot
We miss you so much, our life it is not the same, never will be, we feel cold not hot

As we go through the future without you, your visions will always appear
You were our only son, the one to carry our name, the one we hold so dear
You were our life, someone so special, someone no one can ever replace
It is why day after day, year after year, we will always see your face

Finally, although Aaron is not physically here, he has gone before
We are still very much and always will be, a family of four
His treasured memories, there are so many, will keep him alive
We will tend to his grave, look after him, as long as we are alive

Thank You, To Norma, Aaron's Mum, My Wife

───── ★ ─────

This book could not be completed, without giving his mum a special mention
A devoted mum, who was always there for her son, giving him all her attention
The love she gave to Aaron from birth and through this ordeal was unconditional
She deserves all the accolades, her presence, her contribution, was essential

She endured all the emotions, the highs and lows, which were all part of the agenda
Without her strength of character, from day one, we couldn't have coped without her
She found time to look after her family, throughout this awful period in our life
A wonderful mother, a star like your son, I am so grateful you are my wife

So from me, your husband, I have to say thank you for total dedication
You are an example to us all, for the way you handled the situation
From your family and many other people, nothing but respect is due
Hold your head high, from the beginning to the end, you saw it through

Aaron Final Message From Heaven

—— ✪ ——

These are just a few words that Aaron might say
Now that he has departed this world and gone away
I am sending this message from heaven above
I am happy, I am free and I send you all my love
I am still there in your memories, please don't worry
Please look after yourselves, please don't feel sorry
I want to thank you all for looking after me so well
I have also got a really good secret, I must not tell
The other children must have your total dedication
I have gone, now listen, that is my final instruction
I am up above looking down, watching all of you
Just making sure, all you lot below, carry it through
For all those people I have upset, I must apologise
It wasn't me, it was the drugs, I should have realised
If you are feeling down and having a terrible day
Think of me, I am sure a smile will come your way
The good times with me, will come flooding back
We will meet again, I have only just got the sack
Oh sorry, there is something I forgot to mention
My catchphrase, "Excuse me, can I ask a question?"

THE END

Postscript

───────── ⭐ ─────────

It has given me so much pleasure and yet so much sadness to write this book
At times I have been in tears, my vision blurred, I couldn't see, I couldn't look
But I had to compose these verses, it needed to be completed for Aaron's sake
He is the inspiration, the driving force, if I didn't finish it would be a mistake

To write a complete book of verses has always been my life's ambition
Now to realise it, due to my son's death, fills me with mixed emotions
But it had to be done, his story is worth reading as an inspiration to all
He wasn't very big, but in our eyes and in our minds, he stood really tall

I sincerely hope you have enjoyed reading this book, Aaron's story
Although it is touched with sadness and eventual death, he is covered in glory
I hope it will give you the inspiration in the future, to face life's harsh realities
No matter what your personal circumstances are or whatever adversities

Finally, I ask myself the question and that is why? Oh why?
Why did our only and wonderful son have to die
This question always seems to be on my mind
I search for an answer, an answer I never really find

Thank you

www.marciampublishing.com

BV - #0031 - 270324 - C37 - 254/178/9 - PB - 9781913905880 - Gloss Lamination